Learning Senegalese Sabar

DANCE AND PERFORMANCE STUDIES

General Editors:

Helen Wulff, *Stockholm University* and **Jonathan Skinner,** *Queen's University, Belfast*

Advisory Board:

Alexandra Carter, Marion Kant, Tim Scholl

In all cultures, and across time, people have danced. Mesmerizing performers and spectators alike, dance creates spaces for meaningful expressions that are held back in daily life. Grounded in ethnography, this series explores dance and bodily movement in cultural contexts at the juncture of history, ritual and performance, including musical, in an interconnected world.

Learning Senegalese Sabar

Dancers and Embodiment in New York and Dakar

Eleni Bizas

berghahn
NEW YORK · OXFORD
www.berghahnbooks.com

First published in 2014 by
Berghahn Books
www.berghahnbooks.com

Library of Congress Cataloging-in-Publication Data
Bizas, Eleni.
Learning Senegalese sabar: dancers and embodiment in New York and
Dakar / Eleni Bizas.
    pages cm. -- (Dance and Performance Studies; volume 6)
Includes bibliographical references and index.
ISBN 978-1-78238-256-0 (hardback) -- ISBN 978-1-78238-257-7
(institutional ebook)
1. Dance--Anthropological aspects--Senegal. 2. Dance, Black--Africa,
West--Influence. 3. Dance--Study and teaching--New York (State)--New
York. 4. Dance--Study and teaching--Senegal--Dakar. I. Title.
GV1588.6.B59 2014
792.809663--dc23
                                                            2013022520

British Library Cataloguing in Publication Data
A catalogue record for this book is available from the British Library

Printed on acid-free paper.

ISBN: 978-1-78238-256-0 (hardback)
ISBN: 978-1-78238-257-7 (institutional ebook)

To my grandparents

Άννα και Παναγιώτη Χαλκίδη,

και Ελένη Μπιζά

Table of Contents

Figures

Acknowledgements

This book is the result of a lot of dancing and many discussions. I would like to thank Roy Dilley for reading endless drafts, for his insightful feedback and great support, and for thoughtfully arranging contacts for my fieldwork in Senegal. I would like to thank the series editors: Helena Wulff who provided important guidance at crucial moments and helped me think through different aspects in new ways; and Jonathan Skinner who has been an extremely supportive colleague and a pleasure to work with. At Berghahn Books, I would like to thank Marion Berghahn for her interest, Ann Przyzycki DeVita, Adam Capitanio and everyone else in the production process for their great help. Three anonymous reviewers helped to make this project stronger and I thank them for their comments.

This book owes much to those who inspired it. Jackie Gaffney, a great teacher of West African dances in New York, turned 'tricky' into manageable. My friend Nina shared her excitement of West African dance, and her trip to Guinea triggered this research. I thank all the dancers and teachers in New York and Dakar who took the time to teach me and talk to me, and whose classes I enjoyed so much in all their different ways. While I have anonymized them in this study, I hope they will realize how grateful I am for their help. I would like to thank those I call Issa, Vicky, Marie, Ibrahim, Abdoulaye, André, Michelle, Lisa, Claire and Stella. Michelle's and Claire's insightful reflections on their learning proved imperative for my understanding and subsequent analysis, and Max Goldman's jazz insights helped me to think through my problems with Sabar.

In Dakar I would like to thank Amy, Penny, Emily and Mary for sharing their experiences with me. I thank greatly Mame Bassine Thiam and her family for being excellent teachers and providing me with a fun research environment for fieldwork. I also want to thank Fatou from Les Ambassadeurs who I unfortunately met late in my stay but quickly felt her to be one of my closest friends. I am also extremely grateful to my drum teacher Modou for being so patient, encouraging and protective, and I thank Malal and Hadi Ndiaye for sharing their knowledge of traditional dances. In Dakar I owe a big thank you to Nicole Frossard and her family for easing my arrival and for giving yet another angle through which to look at life in Dakar. I thank the ELI staff at Suffolk University, Dakar Campus for providing a great work environment, and the students for teaching me about their dancing, especially my former students Cheikh Mbaye and Tony Diamanka and my Wolof teacher Mame Binta.

At St Andrews I thank the colleagues from the anthropology department: Adam Reed, Christina Toren, Tristan Platt, Paloma Gay y Blasco, Nigel Rapport, Jan Grill, Lucas Dreier, Ioannis Kallianos, Veronika Groke, Stacy Hope, Maire Ni Mhordha, Daniela Castellanos, Philip Kao, Chris Hewelett, Paolo Fortis, Margheritta Margiotti and Jean Feaux de la Croix. Stephanie Bunn and Stan Frankland provided inspiring talks and important pieces of advice. I thank Kai Kresse for his help in the initial conceptualisation of the project and Huon Wardle for his generous feedback in the final stages. I also thank all the participants of the STAR meetings of the Universities of Scotland for their generous feedback. Parts of this book were presented in the dance panels of the ASA 2009, the EASA 2010 and the AAA 2010, and profited from comments of their participants, especially Brenda Farnell, Helena Wulff and Georgiana Gore.

This research was generously funded by the U.K. Arts and Humanities Research Council (AHRC), the Carnegie Trust for the Universities of Scotland and the School of Philosophical, Anthropological and Film Studies of the University of St Andrews, and I am deeply grateful for their support. The Anthropology Department of St Andrews provided the video recording equipment and the university's IT services generously helped me with video editing. This book includes revised parts from my 2012 article 'Navigating Trans-Atlantic Flows: New York's Senegalese Sabar Teachers, Pedagogies and Notions of Being', published in the *Journal for the Anthropological Study of Human Movement* (*JASHM*) 17(2), and I thank the University of Illinois Press and North American Philosophical Publications for granting me consent to republish sections in this book.

At the Graduate Institute in Geneva, I am extremely grateful to Jérôme Elie and Isabelle Schulte-Tenckhoff for their intellectual support and for granting me access to a great research environment – crucial for the completion of this manuscript. Thank you to Aurélie Mertenat for creating the maps and for coming to my rescue at such short notice! A big thank you goes to all my friends who shared my questions, excitements and anxieties with this project in its different stages, especially Jan Blank, Canan Balan, Anna Glomm, Wies Maas, Björn Remmerswaal and Maria Halkias.

Finally, this book would not have been possible without my family's support. I owe a big thank you to my grandmother Fifi and grandfather Panagiotis Halkidis who inspired my interest in migration, supported me during my studies and empathized with me throughout the completion of this book. My brother Vasilis Bizas stepped in to help me at key moments and I am very grateful. This book owes most to my parents Orea Halkidou and Agapitos Bizas. Their love, unyielding support and encouragement gave me the strength to start, complete and finally publish this project and I cannot thank them enough. Last but not least, I am extremely grateful to Gabriel Geisler Mesevage for his intellectual and moral support, critical reflections and advice, generous proofreading and great understanding.

Figure 0.1 Map of Senegal in Africa
Designed by Aurélie Mertenat for the purpose of this publication

Introduction

Edited Field Notes, New York City, 12 July 2006
The first time in a Sabar class is overwhelming, even for those familiar with West African dances. Nina had warned me. She did not like
Sabar. She couldn't enjoy it. In that first class, I understood why. I
couldn't hear the drumming and couldn't see the movements. Almost
supernatural, lavish jumps; arms flowing up and away from the body;
knees swinging fast to the right and to the left . . . and then a sudden
stop . . . Hips, knees, arms swinging graciously, nonchalant, this way
and that, this way and that, to the right, to the left . . . and then . . .
Jump! Jump! tuuuuuurn . . . Jump! And . . . magically movements end
in a drum-stroke. Magically. With the hip sitting to the right; with the
pelvis pushing forward; with a turn that concludes. Sabar dancers seem
to be playing with a 'momentum'. Transferring waves through the body,
sometimes in unison, others in contradistinction, through the arms, the
legs, the head, the hands . . . But how to start? Following others, I try
to keep up. I jump too early. I come back from a turn too late . . . My
arms rush to complete a move. I miss the accents . . . And then, one day,
the feeling of 'getting it'. 'Filling' time with micro-movements of the
arms, micro-movements of the legs, with a rich turn . . . meeting the
accent of the drum with my hip, meeting the accent of the drum with
the flicking of my wrist . . . The rush of waiting to hear the next accent
as I am almost there . . . The accent. Like the drum-stroke kissing one's
concluding move.

This book is about Sabar, the Senegalese dance and drum form as it is practised in New York City, USA and in Dakar, Senegal. Sabar in Senegal is simultaneously the name of a drum, the name of a family of dance-rhythms and a public dance-event. In New York classes, Sabar refers primarily to the dancing. To avoid ambiguity I will use the word Sabar to refer to the dance form, 'Sabar-event' to refer to performance contexts, and 'Sabar dance-rhythms' to refer to the constellation of dances and rhythms. Over the last thirty years an international network of practitioners has developed around the practice of the West African dances Sabar and Djembé.[1] Here I focus on a loose network that circulates between New York and Dakar. This book is thus also about this network, which I joined as a dance student in New York and methodologically followed to Dakar and back. This movement provided the opportunity to explore comparatively questions of learning and embodiment. Through multi-sited, participant observation and apprenticeship I focused on the pedagogical techniques used in different learning settings in Dakar and New York so as to explore local ideas of learning, being, local aesthetics and forms of dance. As Sabar moves through different settings, it brings together different participants and acquires different meanings in the process. I explored how ideas of learning and forms of dance relate to the socio-economic and political relationships of the participants and the fields they move through.

A Threefold Approach to Sabar

In recent decades, anthropologists have explored local/global connections, have debated how to best conceptualize globalization, and have critiqued its endorsement as a new era by social scientists (Tsing 2000). This work has primarily focused on the socio-political aspects of transnational phenomena. In contrast, the majority of research on embodiment, learning and skill is grounded on one context of practice (Stoller and Olkes 1987, Chernoff 1979, Stoller 2004, Coy 1989, Wacquant 2004, Downey 2005). This book attempts to provide a synthesis of these two areas of research. The transatlantic network of West African dance and a research focus on pedagogical techniques offers the opportunity to explore the socio-political and economic aspects of a transnational process in relation to current debates on embodiment, learning and skill. A focus on pedagogical techniques is a methodological and theoretical shift, which is important for anthropology whose objective is to 'seek a generous, comparative but nevertheless critical understanding of human being and knowing' (Ingold 2008: 69). Exploring how others learn (Dilley 1999b) in turn can help us reflect 'on our own culture-specific ways of conceiving the process of learning' (Dilley 1999b: 34). This transatlantic network offers an interesting setting for such a project as it brings together Euro-American with West African ways of learning in the setting of dance classes. As West African teachers strive to teach and Euro-American students try to learn, the meeting of Euro-American and Senegalese pedagogical techniques highlights differences in ways of learning as well as the paradigms of knowledge that underline them, providing the opportunity to explore local theories of learning while also reflecting on Euro-American assumptions about learning.

Here I approach Sabar in three ways. First, I discuss Sabar-events as social situations within which socio-economic and historical relations are negotiated, and experiential notions, like 'feeling' and 'energy', are defined. I approach learning contexts of Sabar 'dance-events' (Kealiinohomoku 1973, Royce 1977) as access windows to the abstract web of dynamic relationships between participants (Wulff 1998) and as the grounds for the creation and negotiation of meanings (Cowan 1990, Schieffelin 1976). I attempt to investigate how relationships are produced or contested through the dance, through the choice of movements, the use of space and time, the choice of one's dance partners and the choice of dances to teach. The notion of 'dance-event' was offered by Kealiinohomoku (1973) as an entry point for fieldwork that allows the researcher to gradually explore and realize the full extent of the dance activity (Royce 1997: 39). Acknowledging that this does not do away with problems of boundaries, the notion helps to delineate 'the boundaries that are culturally meaningful' (ibid.: 41). In a parallel way to Cowan's analysis of the production and reproduction of gender in Greek dance-events (1990), Sabar-events bring together different participants, becoming the grounds for unequally powerful voices to meet and for relationships to be produced or contested in uniquely bodily ways.

Second, I approach Sabar as a form that provides access to local concepts of pedagogy and dance. These in turn lead to a deeper understanding of local aesthetics and of personhood, or 'being' (Dilley 1999b).[2] I used apprenticeship as a research tool that parallels participant observation at the level of practice and as a method to identify local pedagogical techniques and ideas about learning. Apprenticeship allows the researcher to occupy different positions in the practice (Wacquant 1995), and so through the role of a student, a participant and an audience member I was able to access participants' social relations and construct a general view of the world of the dancers. Learning dance has been a common methodological tool for dance anthropologists who consider it necessary for the anthropologists to gain a better understanding of the form (Kaeppler 1972, Ness 1992, Williams 1997). Through apprenticeship I was able to understand what is involved in performing Sabar in different settings, thus illuminating the different forms that Sabar takes in its transnational and translocal movement.

Third, learning an activity foreign to one's habitual ways of moving provides fertile ground for the exploration of questions of learning and embodiment more broadly. My problems and observations of learning Sabar provided the grounds for comparison with the experience of other students and teachers. As Bourdieu argues, skilled performers may not be able to verbalize their techniques (Bourdieu 1979 and 1990, Wacquant 1995). However, because movements that are opaque to some because they are habitual (Farnell 2000, Ness 1992) can evoke reflection to those not used to performing them, apprenticing in Sabar proved a fruitful way to research what is involved in learning foreign ways of moving.

The approach to this research has been one of 'ethnographic determinism' (Stilitoe 2003: 3), of letting the ethnography determine theory rather than the other way around. This has resulted in this study approaching theory more as a 'fox' rather than as a 'hedgehog' – to evoke Isaiah Berlin's distinction (1953) between writers who relate their work to many theoretical strands as opposed to writers who relate their work to a single theory. By focusing on learning I may not have addressed topics that readers may be anticipating from an ethnographic study of a West African dance, for example race and identity. Such topics, however, in most cases have well-developed bodies of literature, and in delineating a research subject and context one has to make decisions as to what to include and what to exclude (Dilley 1999a).

Theoretical Orientation

In this section I review the theoretical literatures that impinge upon my research domain, and position my work in relation to them.

Transnational and Translocal Moves

This research has been based on multi-sited fieldwork, thus borrowing methods from previous work on translocal and transnational networks of dancers (Wulff 1998), and translocal, yet related, forms of dance (Wulff 2007, Castaldi 2006, Neveu Kringelbach 2005).[3] It differs in that it approaches these networks as the grounds for a comparative investigation on questions of learning. During fieldwork I traced the different forms that Sabar took as it moved through different sites in New York and Dakar by attending classes and by following the people (Marcus 1995), stories, conflicts and relationships – methodological strategies that tend to overlap (Wulff 2007: 142; see also Hannerz 2004). By focusing on Sabar I was in turn able to explore the different socio-cultural settings Sabar moved through (Appadurai 1986: 5). An approach of 'following around' is necessary when exploring 'transnational political, economic, and cultural forces that traverse and constitute local or regional worlds' (Clifford 1997: 27; see also Stoller 1997, Hannerz 2003, Wulff 2000 and 2007: 139–45), forces that eventually merge distinct places into single 'communities' (Clifford 1997: 246), or into a network, as is the case here.[4] Multi-sited research relates to Clifford's articulation of fieldwork as 'travel encounters' (1992), a metaphor which resonates with the nature of this study, as travelling was very much a part of the lives of the students, dancers, teachers, family, friends and myself.

Movement is not new as people have never been static (Gupta and Ferguson 1992, Ghosh 1994, 1998, Mintz 1998). What has recently undergone dramatic change, it is argued, is the speed of the movement of people and information (Appadurai 1990). Appadurai proposed the exploration of 'global cultural flows' through the notion of 'fluid, irregular' (ibid.: 297) scapes, which are 'navigated' by actors, creating new processes and building 'imagined worlds' (ibid.: 296). These scapes, he argues have offered more people to 'consider a wider set of "possible" lives than they ever did before' (Appadurai 1991: 197), thus turning imagination into an important aspect of contemporary life. This study aims to address Appadurai's call for anthropologists to explore the link between imagination and social life by exploring the role that imagination plays in mobilizing U.S. students to visit West Africa, and West African artists to migrate to the U.S. (Chapters 1 and 3). However, I also illustrate the limits of this formulation, as in the movement of Sabar 'centre–periphery' relations (Hannerz 1989, 1997) remain pertinent. Through 'asymmetries of input and scale' (Hannerz 1989: 67), centres (in this case, the U.S.) influence peripheries (in this case, Senegal) in economic and political matters as well as cultural forms (ibid.). The mobility of U.S. students and Senegalese dancers is very much tied to their positionalities in the global economy and thus Sabar is affected by the political geography that the dancers traverse. Centre–periphery relations 'punctuate' boundaries in the transnational movement of Sabar practitioners and consequently in the transnational flow of the form.[5] I offer here an ethnographic account of how socio-economic relationships of participants and the political geography they traverse affect pedagogical techniques and consequently the form of Sabar, aiming to address Tsing's concern that a focus on circulation as the defining characteristic of the global, mistakenly turns our attention to what circulates instead of to the conditions that allow circulation to take place (Tsing 2000: 337).

Furthermore, I explore the ways in which individuals navigate the political geography creatively, negotiating their mobility not only with the government of the host country, but also in the intimate arena of romantic relationships. Imagination is always localized and implicates participants in complex power relations. I explore how imagination takes the form of romance and becomes a very important agent in this network. Arguing against the way relationships in tourist destinations have been theorized as either 'sex tourism' or naïve love (Hall and Ryan 2001, Oppermann 1999, Seabrook 1996, Truong 1990, Ebron 2002, Castaldi 2006), I aim to show the varied and layered understandings and motivations through personal narratives and individual trajectories. I also attempt to represent individual agency as participants negotiate personal desires that are nevertheless grounded within broader socio-cultural fields of meaning. Romance lures some participants to West Africa, but it is also used strategically by others, in the process illuminating complex power relations between North American students and West African artists. This book also aims to contribute to the study of representations of Africa (Castaldi 2006, Ebron 2002, Mudimbe 1988) by providing actors' perspectives on how broad colonial and post-colonial discourses are interpreted on the ground (Chapter 4). While broader discourses are important, individuals have unique ways of conceptualizing their involvement, and so West African dance forms provide the canvas on which participants can project personal desires, grounded within broader socio-cultural fields. Finally, I explore how patterns set in motion in the past have formed avenues towards similar pursuits in the present, adding a historical dimension to the role of the imagination and the global flow of cultural forms (Appadurai 1991).

As Feld and Basso argue, the previous absence of place from ethnographic writing has been replaced with the theorizing of 'its contestation and its linkage to local and global power relations' (Feld and Basso 1996: 4). Here I focus on the geography and politics of the dance floor and following Gupta and Ferguson (1992), who argue for the politicization of the social construction of space, I foreground the discussion with the questions 'How are spatial meanings established? Who has power to make places of spaces? Who contests this? What is at stake?' (ibid.: 11). Spaces and places are political and by 'foregrounding the spatial distribution of hierarchical power relations, we can better understand the process whereby a space achieves a distinctive *identity* as a place' (ibid.). These questions background the discussion in Chapter 2 as the geography of the dance classes and use of space on the New York dance floor provide the grounds for African Americans, other Americans and international students to negotiate the meaning of the class. The classes reflect their geographical, socio-economic and intellectual context, but the dance floor also provides the space for the expression of broader political and socio-economic relations. Tensions are voiced in unique bodily ways in the way space in the geography of the dance floor is negotiated. Participants use the dance floor to re-choreograph larger socio-political relationships and at times subvert larger political and historical relationships.

In its translocal and transnational movement, Sabar moves in and out of the status of commodity. 'Commodity' has been a problematic term (Ferguson 1988, Miller 1995) with most theorists aiming to synthesize the seemingly antithetical notions of gift (Mauss 1922) and commodity exchange (Marx 1887), an antithesis that Hart (1982) argues is simplistic and blurs important commonalities. Appadurai builds on a synthesis of the two and instead turns the focus to the 'social life' of a commodity, whereby its 'exchangeability (past, present or future) for some other thing is its socially relevant feature' (Appadurai 1986: 13). Objects are given historical depth, a life, and so exchange, rather than being an inherent quality of the object, is merely an aspect of its life. Thus commodities are objects that, 'at a certain phase in their careers and in a particular context, meet the requirements of commodity candidacy' (ibid.: 16). So while Sabar's exchange value is highlighted in dance lessons to foreigners in Dakar and New York, and in staged performances internationally, Sabar moves out of the status of a commodity in lay performance settings in Dakar.

The notion of 'authenticity' is an important aspect of Sabar's exchange value as a commodity. Students who travel to West Africa for West African dances vocalize their motives as a search for 'authenticity'. In tourism studies, Reisinger and Steiner distinguish between a modernist, constructivist and post-modernist approach to object 'authenticity' (Reisinger and Steiner 2006a).[6] A constructivist approach considers 'authenticity' to be part of the participants' discourse and not an objective quality of the objects (ibid.). Hosts may reflect tourists' constructs and expectations of what is authentic in their attempt to satisfy these expectations, thus encouraging the persistence of certain traditional art forms and techniques (Cohen 1988 and 1993). Both the artists and students of the Sabar network make claims to authenticity. Since the independence of West African states in the 1960s, politicians and artists have used authenticity strategically to export West African dances as commodities. In addition, in the discourses of international students of West African dance, authenticity appears as a mobilizing metaphor, leading them to take classes and travel to West Africa. 'Authenticity' is also used as a standard in choosing teachers and dances. As Barber argues, however, 'authentic', 'folkloric' and 'traditional' in Africa give clues to the politics surrounding performances rather than to their character (Barber 1987). Thus, authenticity in this book is discussed in the constructivist approach, as it appears at times to be an important category of the participants' discourses, but is not an objective quality of the forms (Reisinger and Steiner 2006a and 2006b). Instead, following Wulff (2007), I maintain that analytically every form is authentic for what it is (ibid.: 18) and thus do not take any form of Sabar to be more or less authentic than any other.

'African Dance' and Dance Anthropology

A comparative approach to dances from Africa is not new. Earlier work explored the retained cultural elements of African dances in the 'New World' (Kealiinohomoku 1976, Sunkett 1995), an approach attributed to Herskovits and his legacy (Kuyk 2003, Ramsey 2000). Written with a political intent, previous research has also highlighted the African influence in U.S. mainstream culture (Dixon-Gottschild 1996, Hazzard-Gordon 1990), an influence that the authors argue remains unacknowledged. This study, however, is less about 'remains' and more about movement and change – movement as danced in Sabar, the movement of Sabar dancers and students and consequently the move-ment of the Sabar dance form between New York and Dakar. The comparative perspective here was also aimed at studying the pedagogical techniques used in New York and Dakar, in an attempt to account for why some techniques persist over others, how these techniques shape different forms of Sabar and why certain learning problems arise as a result of them.

In addition, while there has been a rich literature of excellent historical, politi-cal and socio-cultural analyses of Diaspora dances (Browning 1995, Daniel 1995,

Dobbin 1986, Drewal 1989, Dunham 1969, Malone 1996, Walker 2001, Emery [1972] 1988, Stearns 1994 and DeFrantz 2002), scant attention has been paid to the arrival of West African dances in the U.S. 'as a performance art' (Heard and Mussa 2002). Two recent exceptions are Heard and Mussa (2002) who provide a much-needed historical account of this arrival in the 1950s and distinguish them from Diaspora dances, and Mekuria (2006) who explores questions of U.S. race relations, African American identity, cultural production and authenticity in New York Djembé dances. On the other side of the Atlantic, studies of African art forms have explored the relationship between the arts and performance in regards to religion, politics, tourism, and their representations abroad (Askew 2002, Castaldi 2006, Reed 2003, Gilman 2009, White 2008). This book hopes to contribute to our understanding of who engages with West African dances internationally, how the forms change when transcending different socio-cultural fields and what happens when different paradigms of knowledge meet.

This study relates most directly to the anthropology of dance. Dance appeared early in the anthropological agenda, with Evans-Pritchard writing on it in 1928 and with the first attempt to delineate an approach and objectives for 'dance ethnology' in the 1960s (Kurath 1960). Following subsequent attempts to establish objectives, the anthropological study of dance has inspired a variety of approaches (for reviews see Grau 1993, Buckland 1999a and 1999b, Reed 1998, Kaeppler 2000, Sklar 2000). Perhaps the most consistent thread in this diverse literature has been the problematization of 'dance' as a category (Williams 2004), a response in part to the non-anthropological scholarship on dance. Kaeppler argued that 'we must begin without *a priori* assumptions that dance even exists in the society' (Kaeppler 1972: 173) and in response scholars devised different ways of referring to dance. Williams (1997) and Farnell (1996) consider dance as one of many 'structured movement systems', and Kealiinohomoku (1976) and Royce (1977) introduced the term 'dance-event' as an access window to the 'total range of danced activity' in a different culture (Royce in Williams 1997: 39), which I employed in this study to approach classes and workshops, street performances, private events, public tourist performances and informal learning settings as well as the network of participants. Furthermore, I followed Royce's dual approach to dance (1977): the study of the dances' form and its socio-cultural context.[7] However, I chose not to focus only on Sabar as a dance, which would have entailed a research emphasis on movement at the expense of other aspects that may be important in the practice of Sabar. Instead I chose to employ a methodology that would allow me to unravel the category of Sabar 'from the inside', and so I used apprenticeship to focus on pedagogical techniques instead of movement.

Learning and Apprenticeship

The recent theoretical turn to practice (Ortner 1984) has inspired a number of studies on how bodily forms are learned. Apprenticeship in anthropology has been used as a methodological tool to research communities of practice and to explore questions of learning and enskilment (Coy 1989, Dilley 1989, Wacquant 2004, Stoller and Olkes 1987, Stoller 2004, Chernoff 1979, Pálsson 1994, Downey 2005). Apprenticeship is 'an excellent way to learn a skill or craft or profession', to 'learn about a skill or craft or profession' and finally 'an excellent way to learn about learning' (Coy 1989: 2), and this study addresses these three areas. In this study apprenticeship allowed me to explore Sabar through the pedagogical techniques used in different settings and to locate the practice in its broader socio-cultural, political and economic context. By focusing on pedagogical techniques, instead of movement, I was able to appreciate for example the importance of rhythms, one's attire and facial expression in performing in Sabar-events in Dakar and to delineate how rhythm and movement relate and guide one's improvisational solos. Building on Lave and Wenger (1991) and Ingold (2000),[8] I argue for the need to understand Sabar as a processual and environed activity negotiated with the specific parameters of the performance occasion (Chapter 6). Many scholars have discussed the inseparability of dance from music in African dance forms (Rouch 1972, Rouget [1980] 1985, Kurath 1957: 8, Chernoff 1979, Blacking 1979, Kubik 1979, Locke 1982, Bull 1997, Wober 1991), and this book hopes to contribute to this discussion by delineating the relationship of rhythm and movement in Sabar.

Choosing to use apprenticeship is grounded on the position that it parallels participant observation at the level of practice, giving access to knowledge that cannot be approached otherwise. Sigaut referred to this as the 'implicit' knowledge of skills, and contrasted it to the 'explicit' knowledge, or the information communicated for example in school settings (Sigaut 1993: 106–7), and Polanyi ([1958] 1973) argued that skills in arts, crafts and the sciences are passed on by example and not through 'prescription', which is why they remain out of our awareness: 'by watching the master and emulating his efforts in the presence of his example, the apprentice unconsciously picks up the rules of the art, including those which are not explicitly known to the master himself' (Polanyi 1973: 53).[9] Child development psychologists Vygotsky and Rogoff compared learning through apprenticeship to the way children learn from experience (Vygotsky 1978, Rogoff 1990), arguing that learning happens when one takes a leap between what one knows and what one is called to achieve. In this process guidance from others is necessary as it 'provides bridges between familiar skills or information and those needed to solve new problems' (Rogoff 1990: 66).

Instead of looking for cognitive and conceptual tools and structures to answer how humans learn, Lave and Wenger (1991) shift the focus from the individual learner to the social contexts that allow learning to happen with the aim to translate this into an analytical tool. Learning is located in the co-participation of the apprentice and a 'community of knowledge and practice' (ibid.: 29) within a larger social context. Community for them does not refer to a clearly identifiable bounded group of people of uniform understandings and abilities, and thus extends beyond the master–apprentice relationship and the community of specialists. Learning is processual, 'an evolving form of membership' (ibid.: 53), not in the sense that there is a 'whole' body of knowledge to be acquired but that the apprentice is eventually able to participate 'in an activity system about which participants share understandings concerning what they are doing and what that means in their lives and for their communities' (ibid.: 98). Thus, the apprentice's participation is also shifting: '*Changing* locations and perspectives are part of actors' learning trajectories, developing identities, and forms of membership' (ibid.: 36) which allows members 'to hold different understandings, interests and make diverse contributions to activity' (ibid.: 98). Beyond offering an analytical tool for the study of communities of practice through apprenticeship, Lave and Wenger's theory also accommodates very well the different types of participation in Sabar, that is, the larger community of practice from the lay to the professional dancers in Senegal and the international students in New York.

Apprenticeship, however, is not unproblematic. As Lock argues (1993) the two problems in studying the body are the unknown relation of biology to society and our subjective position – the fact that we are at the same time both the subject and the research tool. The body in anthropology has been approached in many ways (see Csordas 1999, Farnell 1999, Lock 1993), from researching the communicative practices of the body (Hall 1969, Birdwhistell 1970) to how society is reflected on the body (Douglas 1973) and how society 'imposes' itself on the body (Foucault 1980). Mauss was the first to draw attention to the relationship between biology, psychology and society and the idea that bodies are inscribed with habitual movement (Mauss [1935] 1979), suggesting that habits are acquired through mimesis, learning from tradition and explicit instruction (ibid.: 101–2). Here I employ Bourdieu's notion of the 'habitus', a term introduced by Mauss to describe the inscribed bodily practices. The habitus refers to embodied structures that structure our way of acting and experiencing the world, while at the same time recreating these structures. These structures are interrelated and interdependent; they produce and are produced by the social field of the actor as there is a 'dialectical relationship between the objective structures and the cognitive and motivating structures which they produce and which tend to produce them' (Bourdieu 1979: 83). The habitus directs both our social and physical action and, at the level of discourse and practice, the habitus is what allows for communication with other members of society. However, because the habitus is specific to the social fields of each actor, no two people can be expected to act the same way. This gives the 'illusion' of personal style and innovation, which Bourdieu argues is merely the unique combination of socio-cultural fields (ibid.).[10] In this network I have tried both to show how dancers respond similarly to pedagogical techniques based on their socio-cultural background and to account for the ways they respond differently by relating aspects of their individual trajectories that I suggest may partly account for this difference.

Bourdieu calls 'hexis' the habitus of our physical action, which 'speaks directly to the motor-function' (Bourdieu 1979: 87), that is, hexis is passed on at the practical level and never reaches the level of discourse. Even those who have mastered a skill may not be able to identify what underlies their mode of action because 'the principles em-bodied in this way are placed beyond the grasp of consciousness and hence, cannot be touched by voluntary, deliberate transformation, cannot even be made explicit' (ibid.: 94). The habitus, however, can be identified by an external observer (Bourdieu 1990, Wacquant 2004). While this highlights the opaqueness of one's own practice, the process during which a foreign action becomes habitual, and thus moves from intellectual awareness to an 'embodied feel' (Crossley 2004) is gradual and contextual. Furthermore, 'breaks' with one's habitual way of moving create instances for reflection and non-semantic knowledge (Jackson 1983), and 'provoke explicit body awareness' (Leder 1990: 30). Similarly, a trained dancer is more aware of a movement when trying to incorporate it in her routine than when she has practised it for months (Ness 1992) and certain environments such as dance classes encourage explicit awareness. Thus one's ability to reflect on one's bodily hexis is not a static state but a fluctuating process. In certain contexts, the body becomes the focus of monitoring and moulding, in the process exposing a specific bodily hexis. As I illustrate in Chapters 5 and 6, the malleability of pedagogical techniques is linked to participants' socio-cultural trajectories and relationships to others (Bourdieu 1990). Senegalese teachers in New York develop particular methods to accommodate their New York students, while students who aspire to be good Sabar dancers are more reflexive of their practice. I have attempted to illustrate this diversity by including students' voices to show how students employ pedagogical techniques differently depending on their socio-cultural trajectories.

Finally, apprenticeship provides the grounds to compare one's own learning experience with that of others, a limitation to this being that one is restricted from seeing things available to a novice when a practice becomes like 'riding a bicycle'.[11] Apprenticeship allows insight to 'a wide range of feelings and sentiments that are not accessible to outsiders' (Coy 1989: 110). In this case, it helped to illuminate the experiential notions of 'energy' and kinaesthesia, thus contributing to a growing discussion of the senses in anthropology and to what Sklar (2000) has called the kinaesthetic trajectory within dance scholarship. Kinaesthesia, used ambiguously and often interchangeably with proprioception, is 'the reception of stimuli produced within one's own body' (Sklar 2000: 72). Kinaesthesia has been largely absent from a Euro-American understanding of the senses (Sklar 2000 and 2008, Geurts 2002), which instead has treated vision as the most important of the senses (Stoller 1989, Howes 1991, Classen 1993, Ingold 2000). At the same time, scholars on dance and the body have argued that the literature has been dominated by analyses of movement in search of meaning (Novack 1990: 7, Jackson 1983, Csordas 1993). For Jackson the '"anthropology of the body" has been vitiated by a tendency to interpret embodied experience in terms of cognitive and linguistic models of meaning' (1983: 328), a tendency, he argued, that aimed to acknowledge the value and importance of the body by attributing to the body the qualities of the mind,[12] in this sense reaffirming the value of the 'semantic' primarily attributed to the 'mind' (cf. Farnell and Varela 2008).[13] Anthropologists of movement and dance have instead argued that to analyse movement in search of meaning does not do justice to participants' engagement (Downey 2005, Novack 1990) and kinaesthesia has always been important for dance (i.e. Sklar 2008, Potter 2008, Foster 2011).[14] Within anthropology, the growing interest in the senses (Stoller 1989, Howes 1991, Classen 1993, Geurts 2002) has brought increasing attention to the importance of kinaesthesia in certain socio-cultural contexts (Sklar 2000, Potter 2008, Geurts 2002). Kinaesthesia emphasizes the experiential aspect of movement over the visual, and shifts the focus from the observer to the practitioner. It also highlights the importance of the temporality of movement and the experiential aspect of performing. In Chapter 5 I explore the role of kinaesthesia in hindering as well as helping learning, as voiced by New York students. Students discuss the moral feelings induced by certain movements when performed as hindering their learning, which may lead them to avoid certain movements and dances. New York students however also evoke kinaesthesia as an informal, personal learning technique of 'last resort', which they use after all other techniques have failed.

Fieldwork

The fieldwork for this study was multi-sited over a period of fifteen months, six in New York and nine in Dakar. My role was principally that of a Sabar student. I attended an average of four classes of Sabar and Djembé per week. Data collected from dance classes were supplemented with forty semi-structured interviews, informal conversations and data collected from attending performances and street-Sabars. All participants in this study have been anonymized, as agreed in interviews, except for those mentioned in passing. In Dakar, my role as an English teacher also afforded me the alternative perspective of how Sabar and its popular form Mbalax are practised not by professional dancers but by the upper-class Senegalese (see Chapter 1). Due to the transnational nature of Sabar, fieldwork was also multilingual. Data was gathered primarily in English and French, as due to my limited Wolof skills I did not conduct interviews in Wolof. The multilingualism of many of the Senegalese participants proved a major advantage in completing this research.

In New York, the two main research sites were Uptown (East Harlem) where I attended mostly Djembé classes, and Downtown (lower and mid-Manhattan) where I attended mostly Sabar. Uptown classes are primarily taught and attended by African Americans. Downtown classes are taught by West African migrants and attended by an ethnically mixed group of students. Thus the two sites gave me access to very different dance-events and people. It proved much easier to conduct interviews with teachers, dancers and drummers than with students, irrespective of ethnic background. This related to whether or not students viewed themselves as authorities and therefore 'worthy' of representing their dance practice to a researcher. Multi-local fieldwork amongst participants from different socio-cultural backgrounds also highlighted diversity in access and applicability of research techniques. For example time pressures proved a constant concern to most U.S. students in New York, making it much harder to secure interview time after class. In contrast, it was much easier to interview and socialize informally with U.S. students in Dakar. Furthermore, as a white female I was approached differently in the different learning settings. I had easier access to participants in Dakar since I was often seen as a source of income and a potential aid for international travel. In Dakar I was also conveniently placed in the category of a *toubaab* (a person with a Euro-American lifestyle) travelling to Senegal to study West African dance, and thus was generously offered tips and dance moves even by strangers.[15] In contrast, I found it very difficult to gain access to the network of Uptown students in New York, with a few exceptions. The students I did talk to represented a minority in two ways. Firstly, they were experienced dancers and thus saw themselves as 'authorities'. Secondly, they distanced themselves from an 'Afrocentric', *community* sentiment, prevalent among some participants (see Chapter 2).[16] Instead, they viewed the classes as places to advance their dancing skills and thus were more interested in discussing their practice with outsiders. Thus my discussion of Uptown participants is built primarily around the 'authority' figures of advanced students and teachers. Certainly access would have been different had I been an established participant of Uptown classes prior to fieldwork.

In contrast to Uptown students, access to Downtown participants proved much easier. I conducted interviews with all teachers holding regular classes, and with a few who taught occasionally as substitute teachers or as guests in workshops. I interviewed formally and discussed informally with many of the Downtown students. In Dakar I interviewed U.S. students of Djembé and Sabar, some of whom resided in Dakar or were visiting on their way to Guinea. I took classes in two different, broadly defined, learning settings: in classes for foreigners, whose structure resembled New York classes, and in the house of a *géwël* dancer of popular Senegalese music videos. These two contexts produce different forms of Sabar, one intended for international consumption and the other for local consumption. In attending different classes I aimed at cross-referencing in order to identify an individual's personal teaching techniques from the techniques employed more generally by different teachers. In addition to dance classes I took drum lessons in Sabar rhythms, which was important in understanding the relationship of drumming to dancing. Senegalese dancers and drummers have a knowledge of both. In addition to the classes, I attended public and private Sabar-events, dance troupe rehearsals and performances. I conducted interviews and conversed informally with students, dancers of different genres and other authorities.

Finally, a sensitive aspect of any book on dance is the inherent difficulty in communicating its subject in writing (Ness 1992, Sklar 2000, Potter 2008). The same difficulty confronts one as a researcher. The complexity of my learning experience in class was not done justice when recorded as field notes. As a student, it was also impossible to take down notes as things occurred and so all my notes were recorded after class from memory. This also meant that there was an automatic 'selection' as I was able to recall in more detail the information that had left me with a stronger impression, such as the movements that I or others had found most difficult in class, different emphasis on movements from the instructor, unusual social interactions and so on. To monitor my learning and analyse the dance-rhythms I used video recording. This proved very helpful in eliciting feedback from other dancers by playing back performances I had recorded.[17] Videos are also the main medium through which Sabar is diffused nationally and internationally, and so keeping in line with the dancers, teachers and students of Sabar I also encourage the reader to make use of the great diversity of material that is available online.

Movement of the Book

The book is split into two parts; the first provides a historical and socio-cultural background for the network, and the second focuses on learning. Chapter 1 provides a brief historical background to this transatlantic movement of dances from West Africa, and discusses the links of this movement to shifting conceptions of 'caste', gender and learning in Senegal. Chapter 2 takes us to New York and the two different settings for West African dance practice: Uptown and Downtown classes. I explore the reasons for participants' engagement with the dances and how the different understandings and political, historical and socio-economic relationships are re-choreographed on the dance floor. Chapter 3 focuses on the trips to West Africa, from the production of the advertisements to the shifting understandings of the students involved. Chapter 4 explores the different spaces of Sabar dance-rhythms in Dakar and the contesting voices that surround them. The final chapters then focus on the dance-rhythms and explore questions of learning. I concentrate on two common challenges that New York students face in learning Sabar: firstly, acquiring a specific aesthetic quality in their movement, what I call here the 'kinaesthetic of Sabar' (Chapter 5), and secondly, understanding Sabar rhythms and how they relate to movements (Chapter 6).

Notes

1. I have included Djembé in this study because the two forms share performance and learning spaces, are advertised through the same channels and are frequented by the same people in both New York and Dakar. I thus attended classes and interviewed participants of both, which I will refer to as appropriate. Sabar originates from Senegal and The Gambia, while Djembé is practised throughout West Africa – for example in the Casamance (Southern Senegal), The Gambia, Guinea, Mali and Ghana. As Sabar and Djembé transcend national boundaries and are practised by different ethnicities, practitioners tend to use the drum, as opposed to a country or a people, to indicate a dance form. I follow this practice here.

2. I borrow the term 'being' from Dilley's analysis of the Tukulor weavers of Northern Senegal, and apply it in reference to Wolof *géwël*, the 'caste' of the musicians, dancers and praise singers. Similar to the Wolof *géwël*, the 'casted' occupational groups of Tukulor weavers are underlined by 'an indigenous conception of physical and moral constitution . . . which forms part of a cultural discourse about difference or alterity . . . founded upon a series of essentialist claims about who and what members of "caste" groups are' (Dilley 1999b: 46). To practise the occupation of one's 'caste' is seen 'as the outward manifestation of a way of being, not necessarily of a way of learning' (ibid.: 47). Thus, one's 'being' is what marks one as a member of a certain 'caste' and different from others (see Chapter 1 for more on 'caste').

3. I use both 'translocal' and 'transnational' as national borders matter in some cases, while the political geography within one city matters in others.

4. I use the term network over 'community', firstly because community as an analytical term suggests a more bounded entity than is appropriate in this case and secondly because community is a category in the discourses of New York participants and so I maintain its use as such.

5. By 'flow' Hannerz denotes the 'fluent nature of meanings and/or meaningful forms among individuals and social relationships' (1997: 7) and the differential nature of this movement (ibid.: 6).

6. In the modernist sense, authenticity is an objective quality of objects. This leads to the question to what extent tourists can access it, as for example MacCannel (1976) argued that 'authenticity' is rarely experienced by tourists who are merely restricted to pseudo-events and pseudo-experiences. The postmodernist approach renders 'authenticity' irrelevant on the grounds that the concept has ceased to concern the tourists themselves (Reisinger and Steiner 2006a).

7. Royce argued that studies that tend to ignore the dances' form have resulted in 'impressionistic statements about the communicative powers of dance' (1977: 216). On the other hand, analyses of form have often ignored how the dances 'shape and are shaped by cultural standards and values relating to dance' (ibid.: 216).

8. Building on Gibson's 'ecological psychology' (1979), Ingold argues that a person's embeddedness in the world is intrinsic to the practice of a skill. Skilled practice is not only 'the application of mechanical force to exterior objects, but entails qualities of care, judgment and dexterity . . . whatever practitioners do *to* things is grounded in an attentive, perceptual involvement *with* them' (Ingold 2000: 353). As I show in Chapter 6, the pedagogical

and performing guides used in Senegal to communicate rhythm and movement and to improvise on the dance floor highlight the need to conceptualize Sabar as an activity that is carried out through an 'attentive, perceptual involvement' (ibid.) with the different parameters of the Sabar performances, as for example the audience, the rhythm and the nature of the event.

9. Distinguishing between the mutually exclusive *focal* and *subsidiary* awareness of one's actions, Polanyi considered *subsidiary* awareness to be imperative to one's perfection of a skill. When using a hammer, for example, 'I have a subsidiary awareness of the feeling in the palm of my hand which is merged into my focal awareness of my driving in the nail' (Polanyi 1973: 53). If focal awareness is brought to the forefront when one is supposed to be acting through subsidiary awareness, there is a loss of the performance of a skill (ibid.: 56). Polanyi argued that the subsidiary awareness that characterizes our practising of a skill carries on to our improving the skill: 'This is the usual process of unconscious trial and error by which we *feel our way* to success and may continue to improve on our success without specifiably knowing how we do it' (ibid.: 62).

10. Thus for Bourdieu, we always remain and act within the structures of our habitus and as such there can only be 'structured improvisation'. This leads to a common criticism of Bourdieu's habitus, the location of individual agency (c.f. Farnell 2000).

11. I have attempted to represent the fluctuating and contextual understanding of my own involvement through the terminology I use. Having started as a novice of Sabar, the language of my initial involvement includes notions I criticize in my subsequent analysis, most notably in my discussion of the relationship between dancing and drumming. This is an attempt to represent the shifting understanding of my involvement.

12. This is in reference to the Cartesian dualism of mind and body whereby the body is seen as inferior. As Csordas (1994) notes, Descartes is falsely accused of this duality as he introduced it as an analytical tool, never intending it to be an ontological distinction. Leder (1990) argues that this duality persists because even though it is an ontologically ungrounded one, it is nevertheless supported by our experience of ourselves. He believes the positive and negative connotations we attach to our mind and body respectively, are directly linked to the way we experience them everyday. As he argues, we are only reminded of our bodies when they break down, that is when different parts ache and stop functioning the way they are supposed to. In the case of our mind, he claims, there are no comparable cases that may remind us of its existence. This confuses us into thinking that the mind and the body are ontologically different and into seeing the mind as 'immaterial' (Csordas 1994: 8). This experience of ourselves makes us think that the body is something negative, that hurts us, while the mind is superior, always problem free.

13. Jackson's attempt has been criticized by Csordas for not dispensing completely with the 'body as a function of knowledge and thought, two terms with strong representationalist connotation' (Csordas 1993: 136), but is the first comprehensive effort to transcend a representational understanding of movement. Farnell and Varela (2008) argue against Csordas (1990) and Jackson (1983) that semiotic is wrongly conflated with 'representational and/or linguistic' proposing that 'that semiotic can be somatic' (Farnell and Varela 2008: 215).

14. See Foster (2011) for historical perspectives on the different meanings of kinaesthesia in psychology and dance.

15. While confident that my methodology and consistent keeping of field notes set me apart from other dance students, this conviction was challenged by the fact that many U.S. students had spent a number of years in the region and were fluent in Wolof (Dakar, Senegal) and Sousou (Conkry, Guinea), something neither I nor some of the other junior researchers in the area could claim.

16. I am using the term in its local use, to refer to an African American-centric sentiment in these classes (see Chapter 2).

17. I was unable to record all classes in New York, as the U.S. copyright-conscious environment made video recording difficult. I also did not use video recording at some learning contexts in Senegal where the established commodification of dances rendered it unaffordable.

Chapter 1

Transatlantic Travels of West African Dance

West African Dance

> I feel like people lump West Africa together and they're like
> 'Oh, West Africa' or even that it's all Africa!
> They think it's like one country! Which is crazy!
> Mary, Dakar, 2007

'Lumping' West Africa together has been heavily criticized by scholars.[1] In New York, however, the term 'West African' resonates with participants; even with those who have a good understanding of the different countries, peoples and dance traditions, the term 'lumps together', as in West Africa the socio-cultural geography of dances often transcends national boundaries.[2] To complicate matters further, the newly independent states of West Africa of the 1960s encouraged the mixing of dance traditions in their attempts to create unified national identities (Mark 1994). Thus, the same dances are practised in different countries and have often been exported by artists not indigenous to the forms. Furthermore, the primary export sites have been the metropoles – Dakar for Senegal and Conakry for Guinea – which are also the artistically creative centres for the dances to this day. This makes metropoles a significant lieu of origin for the dance forms, in many cases rendering the geographical origins of the different dance traditions of secondary importance. Of the two, Dakar has functioned as the main exporting site of West African forms abroad. But to contextualize the 'lumping' of West African dances and their transatlantic export, some brief remarks on history are in order.

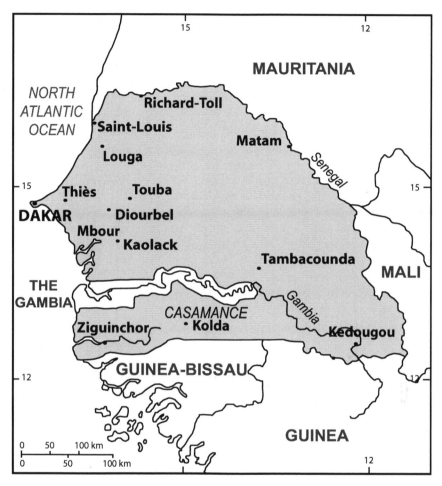

Figure 1.1 Map of Senegal
Map designed by Aurélie Mertenat for the purpose of this publication

> The history of West Africa is the long story of human movements, incursions, displacements, intermixtures or successions of peoples, and of the impact of these on the beliefs, attitudes and social organisation of the various peoples who today inhabit this great area. (Mabogunje 1971: 1)

In this history of movement, Senegal and its capital Dakar have had a unique role in West Africa. This is because of Senegal's special relationship with France during and after colonization. Prior to colonialism, francophone West Africa was engaged in trans-Saharan trade with northern and eastern Africa that was based primarily on the exchange of gold for salt (Davidson 1966: 33). The Wolof Empire in the north of present day Senegal was engaged in trade with Portuguese sea merchants as early as the late 1400s (Davidson 1966). From 1817, France approached Senegal as an important plantation colony and trading post from which it 'hoped to capture the reputedly vast markets of the West African interior' (Newbury and Kanya-Forstner 1969: 254) (see Fig. 1.1). This was despite the fact that French colonies were partly a result of 'individual soldiers, explorers and pioneers . . . who tended to think in terms of square *kilometrage* of land acquired rather than its quality as a sign of success' (Crowder 1968: 75), thus never providing France with the spoils of empire it had hoped for. The state boundaries of present day Senegal, Mali, Guinea and The Gambia were drawn at the Berlin West Africa Conference of 1884–85, generally referred to as 'the Scramble for Africa' (see Hargreaves 1963). From 1885 until independence, French West Africa was administered through common legislation from Dakar (see Fig. 1.1). Furthermore, in contrast to most territories where the French administration governed through a 'paternalistic' approach (Crowder 1968: 171), France applied 'personal assimilation' (ibid.) in Senegal, thus providing the citizens of the four communes of Dakar, Gorée, Saint-Louis and Rufisque the entitlement to French citizenship. Senegal continued its special relationship with France following independence, in contrast to its neighbours. Independence president Senghor had an amicable relationship with the de Gaulle government, in strong contrast to the anti-colonial discourses and practices of the neighbouring presidents of Guinea and Mali, Ahmed Sékou Touré and Modibo Keïta respectively. Since then, Senegal's relative financial and political stability have continued to provide the country with an economic standing that is not shared by its neighbours. Dakar has thus functioned as a centre in West Africa for businesses, non-governmental and international organizations, and has throughout the years attracted migrants from neighbouring countries for work and studies. It has also been a centre of export of West African dance forms.

Independence, Négritude and the Arts

The international export of West African dances has been influenced greatly by the pan-Africanist discourses of the independence governments of West Africa. Following independence, decolonization involved African intellectuals in liberating Africa from the Eurocentric and ethnocentric paradigms that had until then defined the continent as a monolithic, problematic entity. As exemplified in Conrad's *Heart of Darkness* ([1899] 1994), colonial discourses painted Africa as a dangerous, uncivilized, chaotic and savage place: 'For colonialism, this vast continent was the haunt of savages, a country riddled with superstitions and fanaticism, destined for contempt, weighed down by the curse of God, a country of cannibals – in short, the Negro's country' (Fanon 1963: 170). In response, liberating movements endorsed and defended Africa as an entity.

Thus, Senegalese president and poet Léopold Sédar Senghor (1906–2001) and West Indian poet Aimé Césaire (1913–2008) referred to the '*sum of the cultural values of the black world*' (Senghor 1970: 180; italics in original) that should be proclaimed and celebrated as *Négritude*. *Négritude* was 'a rehabilitation of Negro values. The unique contribution of the Negro world to the Western Civilization. Negro Humanism and the need for cultural cross-breeding' (Hymans 1971: 36). Senghor explicitly aligned *Négritude* to other pan-Africanist movements: 'Négritude is nothing more or less than what some English-speaking Africans have called the *African personality*. It is no different from the "black personality" discovered and proclaimed by the American New Negro movement' (Senghor 1970: 179–80). Pan-Africanist movements and intellectuals, like Senegalese historian Diop (1997), have been criticized for defending Africa as a nation and thus maintaining and strengthening racial distinctions by accepting, using and inverting the Eurocentric idea that Western civilization is superior (Appiah 1997, 2001).[3] In their support, Fanon argues that the defence of African intellectuals at a 'race' and a 'continent' level is a natural effect of colonialism:

> The efforts of the native to rehabilitate himself and to escape from the claws of colonialism are logically inscribed from the same point of view as that of colonialism . . . Colonialism did not dream of wasting its time in denying the existence of one national culture after another. Therefore the reply of the colonized people will be straight away continental in its breadth. (Fanon 1963: 170–71)

In contrast to most intellectual debates that remain in the academy, *Négritude* had an impact on the people of Senegal. Senghor's presidential position and love for the arts led him to invest in promoting *Négritude* in Senegal. As African states had no natural unity, Senghor believed the Senegalese people needed a vision to motivate them towards one (Markovitz 1969: 5). The arts were seen as inherently 'African' and as such quintessential in the project of creating a unified national identity.[4] Thus, the performing arts 'received the explicit mission to help construct national or regional consciousness' (Neveu Kringelbach 2005: 196) in Senghor's aim to 'reconstruct the region's "stolen history"' (ibid.). Being part of this agenda, African dance became a medley of different ethnic traditions as artists were encouraged to create and promote a Senegalese national identity (Mark 1994) to be exported to the world for consumption. *Négritude* was in the choreographies, content and structure of Le Ballet National du Senegal and has also had an effect on the choice of dance forms to be exported (Castaldi 2006: 154). As a result, despite the great variety of dance and drum forms in Senegal, the main one to be exported abroad has been Djembé.

In a similar vein but through a different approach, the regime of the first president of independent Guinea, Ahmed Sékou Touré (1958–1984), 'espoused a consistent cultural nationalism, attempting to connect itself with its purely African past, at the same time that it . . . espoused a radical pan-Africanism in the continent as a whole' (Johnson 1978: 38).[5] Differing greatly from Senghor however, Sékou Touré's regime embraced 'scientific socialism and pours scorn upon creeds of "African socialism", "negritude", and the "African personality" as, at best, reactionary mystifications, or, at worst, racism' (ibid.; see also Harshe 1984, Schmidt 2005). Even though Touré distanced himself from Senghor's *Négritude*, Senghor had an important influence on the Guinean elite (Schmidt 2005: 988). In Guinea, artists were seen as the 'cultural ambassadors' to the world, a phrase still popular today, and Sékou Touré invested heavily in the arts.[6] Dancers, drummers and students hail this era as a pinnacle in the history of African dance. This was partly the result of the international exposure that the choreographer Fodéba Kéïta brought to Guinean dance through the creation of Les Ballets Africains while studying in France in 1952. Kéïta 'consciously borrowed dance forms and themes from all the Guinean ethnic groups, blending them into tradition' (ibid.), and the international success led Guinea's politicians to ponder 'the political uses to which such artistic work might be put in the new postcolonial dispensation' (Straker 2007: 211). Mamady Kéïta, a leading drummer of Guinea's National Ballet, Le Ballet National Djoliba, between 1964 and 1979, illustrates the political role of the arts in Guinea:

> In those days, the ballets weren't our idea or our parents. We worked because we had to – for the revolution. The official greeting was 'Ready for the revolution', the reply 'and its demands!' The demands might well be your son or daughter. The revolution chose, not the parents! (*Djembéfola* 1991)

The best dancers and drummers were recruited at a young age from their villages and were trained in the Presidential residence. In Kéïta's words, they were treated as Sékou Touré's children. But as they were part of an important project, the training was accordingly harsh:

> You had to be there at 5.00 A.M. and you couldn't say no unless you were really sick. Balanka Sidiki [the artistic director] was terrible. He gave fifty lashes for the slightest reason. We formed a delegation to tell the governor that he [Sidiki] was too tough. The delegation was immediately arrested and handcuffed, and the rest of the troupe was thrown in jail! (*Djembéfola* 1991)

Balanka Sidiki's response to this: 'Our duty was to develop the national spirit!' (ibid.). The legacy of Sékou Touré is alive today, and U.S. students make references to his era to describe a dancer's quality:

Oh! She was handpicked from the Boké region and I don't know how old she was when they scouted her out but she was basically not even a teenager, probably 12! (Amy, Dakar, 2007)

One of the leading elders of the dance and music tradition in Guinea. He's got all the knowledge during the time of Sékou Touré . . . Anyone who trained during that time, they are the pure, they have the purest sense and knowledge of the dance and music, and those are the people who I look for in terms of getting the stories and the history, and their students are usually who I dance with, in terms of who I want to teach me, I want people from that training, from that era! (Penny, Dakar, 2007)

Exporting Dance

It was terribly hard, but if the revolution hadn't taken me from the village I'd still be scratching the earth with my brothers . . . it is because of a piece of wood and a goatskin that I have a better life today. (Mamady Kéïta in *Djembéfola* 1991)

The growing international success of African music and dance, the international tours of ballets and the quality of artists' training promised artists a life out of Africa and out of poverty. The greatest international migration of Senegalese artists took place in the mid-1980s (Neveu Kringelbach 2005) but not many Guinean artists were able to follow. Guinea's political and economic standing gave its artists limited access to the world.[7] Instead, many of them migrated to Senegal's more stable political and economic climate,[8] a migration that continues to this day and has contributed to the international export of Guinean dances by Senegalese artists.[9] U.S. dancer Emily described to me an example of this exchange between Guinea and Senegal in relation to West African dances. Emily used to perform in the U.S. with a group founded by a Senegalese drummer. In one festival where they performed Emily remarked on a shocking resemblance between the choreographies of her group and another group directed by a Senegalese dancer. In her words, their repertoire was 'stolen' from the Senegalese dancer with whom their director had trained. As creative authorship has different significance in West Africa than in the Euro-American context, upon discussing this similarity with the other director he explained to Emily that the choreographies were passed on from one person to the next. He himself had learned them in Senegal from a Guinean dancer who had spent many years teaching others in Dakar and Saly (south of Dakar).

The Djembé stuff is pretty much borrowed from Guinea and there's been an exchange over the years between the two countries, from Guineans leaving Guinea to come to Senegal to Dakar to have more opportunities, because you know, Guinea was pretty closed for a while, less developed, less opportunities for travelling. (Emily, Dakar, 2007)

Thus Guinea's and Senegal's links during and following colonialism have sustained an exchange between the two countries, privileging Senegal as the premier West African site for the export of West African dances. This has also enabled Senegalese to export Djembé, which remains the most popular West African dance internationally.[10]

African dance arrived in the U.S. 'as a performance art' in the 1960s during a period of upheaval in both the political and dance scenes, a period that DeFrantz argues (2002) is poorly documented, complex and difficult to write about today. African American dancers like Katherine Dunham, Alvin Ailey and Pearl Primus brought the African, African American and African Diasporic presence closer to the U.S. audience, on a stage previously dominated by white performers.[11] The broad reception of African dances in America was linked to the Black Power movement (Heard and Mussa 2002), a time when African American youth was 'in search of self-discovery' (ibid.: 146) and African dance 'offered the recognition of an ancient, pre-colonial self and was supported as a viable vehicle of cultural revolution by leaders of the Black Power movement' (ibid.). Out of this era came the Chuck Davis Dance Company founded in 1968, the first African American dance company to perform exclusively West African dances on stage. During this period African dance classes and performances became 'staples of African American political events' and 'community centre programming' (ibid.: 146). Since then, many African American companies perform traditional African movements or combine them with modern dance elements. The one with the strongest presence today is Abdel Salaam's New York-based Forces of Nature.

In documenting the twentieth-century arrival of dances from West Africa to New York, Heard and Mussa (2002) define them as 'performance art' to distinguish them from Diaspora dances.[12] The first 'performance art' troupe to arrive in New York was the group of Nigerian Efrom Odok in 1921. Dances from Guinea arrived in the 1950s with Les Ballets Africains, and Heard and Mussa identify Ladji Camara as the man responsible for bringing Djembé to the United States (2002: 143). Since then, the predominant African dancing traditions practised in New York City are those of the Old Mali Empire of the Manding, or the Malinke/Bambara-speaking peoples (Djembé) (ibid.), which remains the case today. My interviewees placed Sabar's arrival in New York to the late 1980s, which coincides with the period of the biggest wave of Senegalese migration to New York (Perry 1997: 229).[13] I found no agreement as to who was the first Sabar teacher in New York but was given the names of Amadou Boly, Batou Samba, Marrie Basse-Wiles and NDeye Gueye, the last two of whom are still teaching today.

John, a long-term student of Djembé and Sabar, remembers Soho and Manhattan's Lower East Side in the 1980s full of African and Diaspora dance classes.[14] Katherine Dunham's technique had popularized Haitian dance in New York, which according to John increased the demand for classes taught by migrants. This trend was taken up by dance studios which had West African and West Indian migrant teachers for their classes. In the years that followed, however, studios did not survive the rising cost of Manhattan real estate and were forced out of business, leaving only one studio in Manhattan devoted to 'exotic' dances at the time of this fieldwork. West African classes in New York also triggered the movement of U.S. students to West Africa. In recent years Djembé and Sabar teachers have organized two- to three-week-long trips to Guinea and Senegal to provide their U.S. students with a contextual understanding of the dances. Many classes in New York are still listed as 'West African' or simply 'African', but increasingly they are specified by the main drum used or by the dance's region of origin (i.e. Sabar, Congolese, Djembé), which also reflects growing preference for some styles over others.

Dancing Bodies, 'Caste' and Authority

How has the transatlantic movement of the dances and artists affected ideas about Sabar in Senegal? For the Wolof of Senegal, dancing, drumming and praise singing have traditionally been the cultural capital of the 'caste' of the *géwël*.[15] However, the international demand for West African dances has led many non-*géwël* to engage with dance as a profession as it promises a better life in Senegal and abroad. This in turn creates tensions between *géwël* and non-*géwël*, who make claims to authority over the dance forms on different grounds.

Although the term 'caste' is problematic for the West African context (Dilley 2000, Tamari 1991, Wright 1989) it is still used conventionally, both locally and by scholars, to refer to endogamous groups of artisans, musicians and praise singers. By being born into a 'caste', one is assumed to have a 'natural' predisposition to one's family occupation, even if one does not practise that occupation later in life. 'Castes' can be found throughout West Africa (Tamari 1991: 221) and there is considerable debate as to how they should be conceptualized. According to Panzacchi (1994), Wolof society can be divided into three hierarchical stratifications: the *géer* (freemen, un-casted), the *ñeeño* (artisans and griots) and the *jaam* (slaves). The *ñeeño* compose ten to twenty per cent of the Wolof population (Tamari 1991: 224) and include the *géwël* musicians, praise singers and dancers along with artisan groups of leatherworkers, blacksmiths and weavers. The *ñeeño* 'were free but not in control of land distribution [or] therefore the decisive means of political control' (Panzacchi 1994: 190). Abdoulaye-Bara Diop (1981) offers a different version, identifying two coexisting classifications in Wolof society: the first, the 'castes', are based on professional occupations, while the second, the 'orders', are defined by political power (Diop 1981: 33–34). Both describe distinct social categories that nevertheless influence each other. The 'castes' are composed of the two binary opposites, the *géer*, which he calls the superior 'caste', and the *ñeeño*, the artisans. In contrast to Panzacchi, Diop sees the relationship of the *géer* and the *jaam* (slaves) as determining social power, from which the *ñeeño* were excluded.[16]

The above scholars emphasize the 'castes'' hierarchy and social inequality (Irvine 1974, Diop 1981, Tamari 1991). Others however highlight local discourses of power and difference, and advocate for an understanding of how the different groups are interrelated (Wright 1989, Dilley 2000). Wright argues that the distinctions amongst the Wolof are 'best understood as a set of groups differentiated by innate capacity or power sources' (1989: 42). This perspective, she says, illuminates the way different groups are related while also allowing the framework of the 'caste' to be one amongst many through which one's power and identity are defined in relation to others such as ethnic groups, descent, gender and place of origin. However, while one's 'ethnic identity . . . is open to manipulation and change . . . "caste" is immutable' (Wright 1989: 47). In relation to Tukulor weavers, Dilley concludes that 'an indigenous discourse of . . . alterity or difference is symbolically elaborated in terms of bodies of knowledge and competing systems of power, as well as with reference to racial distinctions' (2000: 149). He argues for an understanding of 'castes' as 'social ranks' and 'social categories', where 'social ranks' refer to the position of each group as for example the nobles or the uncasted, craftsmen, musicians, dancers and praise singers and finally bondsmen and bondswomen, while 'social categories' refer to the hereditary endogamous occupational groups (Dilley 2000). In reference to the Mandé (related ethnicities including the Manding, Malinke, Bambara and Djola) Conrad and Frank argue that in order to understand how individuals 'play on the politics of power and difference that inform virtually all social interaction' (Conrad and Frank 1995: 12), we need to acknowledge that the perspective through which we approach the caste system will influence how it looks. As such 'men-of-skill tend to emphasize connections of complementarity within a social division of labour, whereas freemen highlight ties of dependence and hierarchical differentiation' (Dilley 2000: 155). The formulations of Wright, Dilley, Conrad and Frank seem most appropriate in explaining the way dancers in Senegal claim authority over dancing.

The relationship between the *géwël* and the *géer* is one of interdependence. The *géwël* exercise their power to praise a certain *géer*'s generosity and ancestors, by thus raising his status publicly. This forces the *géer* to prove his generosity publicly by giving the *géwël* gifts and money: 'the size of the recompense is contingent upon the ability of the individual(s) to pay and upon the quality of the services rendered' (Wright 1989: 49). Failure to do so leads to the public insult and embarrassment of the *géer* since 'the *géwël*'s tongue, after all, far more than the *géer*'s, is thought to have the power to ruin a person's reputation, and consequently his life and posterity' (ibid.). Today, the *géwël*'s dependence on the *géer* for money has been broadened and adapted to accommodate contemporary opportunities (Panzacchi 1994). As such, applying the same methods to elicit money, the *géwël* will praise anyone 'who is, or wants to be, or whom they want to make believe is, their social superior' (ibid.: 195), a practice which has been extended to include *toubaabs*.

Dancing Professionally

So how has the professionalization of dance affected traditional ideas of 'caste'? As dancing has become a profitable occupation, a *métier*, the moral qualities once linked to the occupation of the *géwël* are now of secondary importance. Non-*géwël* now also claim the cultural capital that was once the exclusive trait of the *géwël*. Thus the *géwël*'s social status is not as important as the body of knowledge pertaining to dance. Traditionally, *géwël* occupations carried negative connotations and were avoided by the *géer*. Stories about dancers involved drugs, alcohol, loose morals for the women and homosexuality for the men: 'Oh, people would say before "I'm not gonna let my kids get into art, then they'll become gay" . . . that kind of thing, or if it's a woman, "Oh, she's gonna be like a bad woman, she won't care"' (Ibrahim, New York, 2008). Concerns were often voiced from the dancers' parents wanting to protect their children's reputations. These concerns however disappeared once a dancer was an established, successful artist. Youssou NDour is a prime example of this. According to Youssou NDour's sister: 'our parents didn't want him to sing . . . because at the time musicians in Senegal were not successful, they didn't make much money and had a reputation for drinking alcohol' (Duran 1989: 278). Similar negative remarks accompanied the early careers of many of the dancers I interviewed. They did not discourage them however from pursuing dance professionally.

More recently, dancing is being seen as a viable source of income and approached as such by *géer* and *géwël* alike. Panzacchi locates this shift in the 1960s, and attributes it to recent generations' tendency 'to romanticize the profession of griot, associating it, on one hand, with an unalienated, "authentic" pre-colonial Africa and, on the other, with a relatively easy access to a promising career as a musician' (Panzacchi 1994: 200). The ballets promise – even if rarely deliver – a regular income through festival and hotel performances. For example, Lamine, a *géer* Senegalese dancer envisioned of becoming a professional jazz dancer. He thought that the best way to gain a living from dance was as a dancer of traditional ballets.[17] Through rigorous training he landed a spot in Le Ballet National du Senegal, where dancers receive a government salary. Following his career in a traditional ballet, Lamine joined a contemporary dance company only to later move and teach traditional dances in the U.S. This trajectory is not rare as, other than providing a regular income, traditional ballets also breed dreams of travel, which at times materialize and lead to a life abroad.[18] Both are strong incentives to pursue dance professionally:

Now most of the people dancing and drumming are not even *griots*. Before, when I was growing up, if someone dancing and drumming was not *griot*, it was really bad. Now they're just doing it to get out of Senegal. (André, New York, 2006)

The ballets are also seen as opportunities to expand one's knowledge of ethnic dances. As the *géwëls'* knowledge is profound but limited to their own ethnic tradition, ballets offer the opportunity to expand one's repertoire and thus become a more competitive dancer in the traditional ballet world (Castaldi 2006: 157). As a *géwël* explained:

For me, the ballet is something you go to practise in. In the Sabar [event] you don't go [to] practise. You perform what you know. But the best thing for me is the ballet because the more you practise the better you are. So mostly, most of the griots, they don't go to the ballet to learn, they just go to the ballet to learn choreographies, because you don't learn something you have in the blood. (Ibrahim, New York, 2006)

Even though dancing is now seen as a profession, traditional conceptions of 'castes' are still relevant. In fact the cultural capital of the *géwël* is very much prevalent in the way *géer* and *géwël* dancers present themselves and the way they make claims to authority.

Abdou Ba, a dancer with a long career in performing and training dancers for ballets, explained:

A: The griots and the artists are different. The griot is not necessarily an artist and an artist is not necessarily griot.
E: Are you from a griot family or are you an artist?
A: No I'm not from a griot family, I'm an artist. I come from a family very noble, because before, in our family line, we had chiefs of districts. Normally if those stories worked until today [if that was the way things were done today] it would be me the chief of those districts.
E: Because I was told that before not many people danced if they were not griots.
A: No, it's not true, it was always like this. Before, we would call them Mbandaankat. They are artists. At the end of every summer, the villages would organize celebrations under the moon and they would dance, would tell stories, all that . . . it was like the Troubadours. That always existed in Senegal. (Abdou Ba, Dakar, 2007)

Neveu Kringelbach traces the term 'Mbandaankat' to 'dancers and bards who celebrated the beauty of young women and were paid in return', and who –

according to her informant – can be considered the '"ancestors" of today's professional dancer' (Neveu Kringelbach 2005: 83–84). Above, Abdou Ba presented
himself as an 'artist', as many dancers do, thus circumventing the connotations
of the *géwël* while claiming authority over the dances on different grounds than
those defined by the *géwël*. By linking 'artist' to Mbandaankat, Abdou Ba makes
claims to authority on traditional and historical grounds. He thus circumvents
géwël's authority while at the same time appropriating some of the very grounds
for this authority: tradition and history. By presenting themselves as 'artists',
non-*géwël* also make claims to 'professionalism' which they claim the *géwël* lack.
Thus, while traditionally a 'caste' occupation of the *géwël*, the international
success of traditional dances and dancers has attracted *géer* into the profession.
Instead of shifting traditional ideas about 'castes', this has given rise to new
grounds on which to claim authority over the dance forms.

The Dancing Body

Linked to how 'castes' are conceived are traditional notions of being, of knowing
and learning:

> Indigenous ideas about ancestry, stock, and so on, therefore, compose an
> essentialist discourse about cultural identity, such that members of social
> categories are held to possess specific qualities . . . These qualities are the
> bases of an elective affinity or predisposition members of a social cat-
> egory have in relation to their specialist occupation. (Dilley 2000: 161)

Other than having access to a specific body of knowledge, Dilley argues that
'caste' should also be considered a synonym of race, as '[t]he distinctiveness of
each social category is expressed in the sense of a separate ancestry, breed or stock
or race' (Dilley 2000: 159). This ancestry is thought to provide the members of a
'caste' with the predisposition to one's occupation. The most common expression
of this among Senegalese dancers is that dance is 'in their blood'.[19] To understand
the importance of ancestry in Senegalese hereditary groups and the claims of difference based on lineage, Dilley uses Appiah's distinction between racism and
racialism as the two different doctrines of nineteenth-century thought (Appiah
1992). Racialism is grounded on the notion that 'All members of these races
share certain traits and tendencies with each other that they do not share with
members of any other race . . . [that] constitute . . . a sort of racial essence' (ibid.:
19). Racialism can provide the grounds for racist action when racialist ideology is
employed to implement social inequality. Racialism however does not necessarily
become the grounds for discrimination 'provided that positive moral qualities
are distributed across the races, each can be respected, can have its "separate but
equal" place' (ibid.). Essential differences in Sabar point to local conceptions of
'caste' as an essential alterity, close to Appiah's definition of racialism. How do
ideas of essential alterity relate to dancing and learning to dance Sabar?

'In the Blood' and 'In the House'

The traditional learning setting for dancing and drumming is the *géwël* household. 'The family is of central importance to Wolof *géwël*, fostering the production and reproduction of *géwël* knowledge' (Tang 2007: 57). *Géwël* dancers will often claim authority on the basis of the traditional conceptions of 'caste', quoting that dance is in their blood:[20] 'It's in my blood, I cannot stop . . . it is in my blood, that's why . . . my family , my dad is *géwël*, my mom is, my grandfather . . . all of them *griot*' (Abdoulaye, New York, 2006). This quality does not determine one's skills in dancing, but *géwël* dancers are assumed to have a natural predisposition to being better dancers than non-*géwël*. However, beyond essential, natural differences, dancing skills are also discussed as a result of the environment, of an upbringing in a *géwël* household:

> Like me, my family, everywhere you go at the house, you see someone drums, so you always pass by and play and go and play and go, you know? [laughs] and they play music, and your big brother, your big sister dancing and you see them dance, then you start doing step by step, you grow up with it. (Abdoulaye, New York, 2006)

The same rationalization for *géwël* skills is also found in the literature: 'they are brought up in a family where music, dance, drumming and praise singing are part of everyday life' (Panzacchi 1994: 199). The *géwël* household is an authority context for learning and is evoked as proof of one's abilities, by *géwël* and non-*géwël* dancers alike. *Géer* dancers for example may recount how they grew up next to a *géwël* household or had *géwël* friends, thus linking their dancing skills to spending time in the authority learning setting of a *géwël* household. Professional dancers also evoked the importance of the environment in learning Sabar. For example a male dancer once refused to introduce me to a female member of his dance company for an interview on the grounds that she had not been raised in the *quartiers*, the districts of Dakar. He argued that the dancer's father's frequent travels to Europe had given her access to a different life and education, a cultural capital that set her apart from the women of the *quartiers*. The *quartiers* are important as they are where street-Sabars take place and where children learn by observing and imitating the dancers in the circle. The *quartiers* are where lay dancers learn.

Yet, views on the importance of the environment were not consistent. Some *géwël* for example argued that no matter how well a *géer* may train, there would always be something lacking. They might not be good at improvising for example. Yet others believed that anyone could learn to dance and that while they can usually recognize one's 'caste' from one's dancing, there are times that they are unable to do so:

You're not born to do the computer, but when you go learn, you will do your best. People go to learn all the time . . . That's why sometimes I see a person who is not griot and they dance very well! They dance very well because they learn to do their best, and put their energy inside and do it! But sometimes I see the difference . . . I see the difference . . . I can know a lot of things they don't know. Because I'm . . . it's my culture [as *géwël*].[21] (Abdoulaye, New York, 2006)

This analogy between learning computer skills and *géer* learning to dance emphasizes how extrinsic dancing is thought to be to the nature of the *géer*.

Gender, Age and Physique

In addition to local notions of predisposition, one's dancing is also affected by one's gender, build and age. A contemporary dancer told me that today's Sabar cannot be considered traditional, even if the movements are identical, because of the different physique of the bodies performing it. The 'ancestors' were stronger as they engaged in a lot of physical work working in the fields, he argued. Today's men are not as strong, and so while the movements may be the same, the bodies performing them are not. Sabar today is a different dance. As in many other dance forms, one's physique affects one's dancing. Yet, while in the Euro-American dance tradition one's body is discussed as a project to be worked on and altered (Wulff 2002: 74), that is not the case for lay Sabar dancers.[22] Ideas about physique are so important in Sabar that one's gender, age and build are thought to lead dancers to perform differently. Consequently certain dances are seen as more appropriate for some dancers than for others.

As such, *ceebujen*, a very fast dance-rhythm that requires a lot of jumping is considered to be a dance for younger women. In contrast, *baar mbaye* is for older women, or 'those who cannot jump', where one's curves are an important aesthetic quality of the movement. As older women in Senegal tend to have fuller figures, *yabba* – a dance-rhythm similar to but slower than *baar mbaye* – is played when there are older women attending. Similarly, women with more curves are also thought to be better dancers of *lëmbël* as the subtle movements of the dance are magnified when performed by a fuller figure: 'If you have a big bum you can dance *lëmbël* well!', I was once told by a taxi driver. Thus differences in tempo and movements make certain dances more appropriate for some women than others. These distinctions are not so rigid that women refrain from dancing a rhythm not considered appropriate for their age. Rather, drummers use them as general guidelines to adjust the repertoire to the audience of every Sabar-event. They will thus play more *baar mbaye* and *yabba* if the majority of attendees are older women but more *ceebujen* if there are mostly younger women dancing. While discussions about age seem to relate to one's physique, the articulated differences on the grounds of gender point to something important about Senegalese notions of 'being'.

Distinctions on the grounds of age and physique were not articulated for male dancers. This is because Sabar is generally considered to be a female dance with many Sabar-events taking place in private settings with an exclusively female audience. In contrast, most of the men who dance do so professionally, and so abide to Euro-American standards of build. The more exclusively female events are called 'tours'; they are organized by women's associations and often feature the most provocative dancing.[23] However, they are not exclusive to women as the drummers are always male. Sabar-events that take place in the streets of Dakar are semi-public and thus may include men as both dancers and/or onlookers. These are organized for naming ceremonies, marriages and political meetings, and may also be held by anyone who can afford to organize them.[24] However, even in these cases it is mostly women who perform short, improvised solos in front of the male drummers.

I first became aware of the importance of gender in Sabar following some lessons with a male dancer named Tony. Tony had taught me a short choreographic sequence, and then one day a female teacher substituted for Tony and asked me to show her what I had learned. When I finished my dancing she repeated the moves, instructing me to make them subtler and at times giving me alternative movements for some of the ones that Tony had taught me. She explained that Tony is a man, and 'men are robust and do "big" movements'. What was interesting was that Tony is a thin man of small build, smaller than both the teacher and myself. So it was not Tony's physique but something inherent in Tony's 'maleness' that guided my female teacher's instruction. As a male teacher in New York in 2006 put it: 'Men and women are different. There are different moves women do in Sabar, we men we don't do . . . We try to do and a lot of stuff we do, good stuff, but you can still tell you know . . . When the woman does it you can tell the difference'.

A Senegalese drummer told me that because 'humanly' men and women are different, men could never perform the movements like women do, even if the movements are identical. A male dancer similarly explained that even if a man can 'catch' a movement and imitate it exactly, he 'cannot do [it] all the way like a woman'. A man may teach the movement to others but 'still something is gonna be missing'. According to him, distinctions between men and women are a result of difference in 'nature'. Men, he said, are 'physical, powerful' because of their 'hormones' and this explains why men dance with acrobatic movements and use their legs more. Instead, the nature of women was said to be 'playful, sensual, harmonic', which explained the gracious movement of their hips and their use of the arms: 'The woman is love, with their body that plays, with their elegance that plays, when they dance you see a body, which moves with love. A man with his hormones . . . when he starts doing Sabar his physicality enters the dance' (Senegalese drummer, Dakar, 2007).

The above suggest a difference in 'nature', which other dancers described as 'style':

(a) They're different, because men's style is different from women's. The men's dancing nowadays is heavier. Women dance like women, more like hand and stuff, [while] men dance more with their legs. (New York 2008)

(b) The way they dance is different because of power. Men dance with more power, stronger, but some women dance stronger than the men – it depends how you feel the rhythm in yourself, your style and all that. (New York, 2008)

Here the idea of style seems to refer to movements that are characteristic of a male or a female repertoire, but 'style' was also used to refer to individual ways of dancing. It is not that male and female bodies are that different but that individuals have different 'styles' in dancing.

The above discourses point to certain essential differences between men and women that are deemed unbridgeable. They outline general expectations of male and female dancing such that acrobatic, powerful movements are characteristic of male dancing while gracious movements of the hips and arms are a trait of female dancing. This does not mean that people refrain from using certain movements. In fact men often trigger laughter from the audience by imitating women. Similarly, professional female dancers will often incorporate acrobatics and large movements in impressive solos. In those cases however they are seen to have appropriated female movements: 'You see some men dance like women', which the dancer justified in terms of physical build:

The way the body is built up too. You see some men, [how] they dance, [and] you will think 'Wow they're women'. You can tell from a lot of teachers, you've been around, you take [a] lot of classes, you can tell who has kind of female movements, or masculine. (Ibrahim, New York, 2008)

Sometimes the difference is attributed to the dancer's upbringing:

Some women dance more than men. I used to dance with a woman who danced like a man. When she danced you think it's a man. She had dreadlocks too. She never braided her hair, she just left it like that . . . She grew with the boys, the same area, everybody danced and she was the only girl. She did everything with them. (Assane and Moussa, New York, 2008)

This emphasizes the influence of one's environment on one's dancing, taking us back to the importance of the *géwël* household.

Dancing like someone of the opposite sex was often discussed as one's environment rubbing off on one's dancing. This was also the prominent explanation when I enquired about how a *goorjigeen* (manwoman) dances:

> They say homosexuals dance like women, if you can tell women and men dance differently, homosexual is gonna be man but is gonna try to dance like a woman. I would say there is a difference there . . . Yeah, in Senegal there are many *goorjigen* by name; they act like *goorjigen* but they are not. They just act because a lot of them just grow up with the women especially ones that grow up with families and like to hang out with the women all the time. Some of them don't know that they talk like women, or they act like women. (Assane and Moussa, New York, 2008)

The assumed differences between dancers' inherent potentiality are thought to be observable in the dancing of *géwël* and non-*géwël*, men and women and in different age groups. The essential potentiality however is also seen to be malleable by one's environment. Thus there are also assumed restrictions on what one can learn and perform. When a movement is replicated, it is expected to evince the dancer's age, body and gender. These traits, or 'style' as some dancers described it, are not always possible to overcome. 'Style' is so important that it defines one's ability to be a good Sabar dancer.

So how do ideas about alterity, predisposition and environment translate in Sabar's transnational travels? The idea that men cannot dance like women is largely ignored in the New York setting, where most teachers are male and the students are female. During the fieldwork of this study, there were three male teachers holding regular classes while two female teachers taught occasionally in workshops.[25] While in the daily classes the significance of gender was ignored, in workshops with female 'guest teachers' gender was often advertised: 'You know there is only so much we can teach you as men'. Similarly, ideas about alterity were extended to foreigners. Thus some movements are considered problematic for *toubaabs*. My teachers in Senegal assessed my dancing in relation to this, informing me when they expected me to have trouble with certain moves. At times my inability to perform them confirmed their expectations, while at other times it was met with remarks of surprise: 'you do it better than most *toubaabs*'.

Thus 'caste', gender, age and physical build are seen to influence one's dancing abilities in Sabar, and so certain dance-rhythms are considered to be more appropriate for some dancers than others. These differences point to conceptions of essential alterity that resonate with Appiah's racialism. However, the post-independence export of Sabar and the transatlantic movement of its practitioners have led dancers to engage strategically with traditional ideas about who can dance. Thus *géwël* and non-*géwël* dancers claim authority to dance forms on different grounds, and approach traditional ideas instrumentally, ignoring them or advertising them depending on their audience.

Notes

1. There is also evidence of 'lumping together' from migrant communities themselves. In what is considered to be the first and largest study of West African migration (Stoller 1992: 77), Jean Rouch (1956) found that migrants from the Sahel to Ghana would set aside distinctions made on ethnic and sub-ethnic grounds that were important in the North and would instead use new categories to describe themselves that were made on geographical grounds (Stoller 1992: 70).

2. The following figures indicate how ethnicities and consequently dance-rhythms transcend West African state borders: **Senegal**: Wolof 43.3%, Pular 23.8%, Serer 14.7%, Jola 3.7%, Mandinka 3%, Soninke 1.1%, European and Lebanese 1%; **The Gambia**: Mandinka 42%, Fula 18%, Wolof 16%, Jola 10%, Serahuli 9%, other 4%, non-African 1% (2003 census); **Guinea**: Peuhl 40%, Malinke 30%, Soussou 20%, smaller ethnic groups 10%; **Mali**: Mandé 50% (Bambara, Malinke, Soninke), Peul 17%, Voltaic 12%, Songhai 6%, Tuareg and Moor 10%, other 5% (The World Factbook 2009, accessed 19 March 2011).

3. For Diop (1997), ancient Greek civilization, and consequently Western civilization, was based in ancient Egypt, and 'ancient Egypt was a Negro civilization'. Appiah (1997) however argues that in Diop's desire to claim a right over 'Western civilization', pan-Africanists have bought into what Europeans have been promoting. For Appiah, pan-Africanist movements do not provide alternative paradigms as they assume and maintain 'natural' racial distinctions that hinder cooperation towards a new 'basis for political action' (Appiah 2001: 228). He argues instead for a pan-Africanism that recognizes the distinct socio-economic formations of many African identities and does not merely blend them all into race (ibid.).

4. The political use of the arts is not restricted to West Africa but is a general feature of nationalist movements (see Askew 2002, Daniel 1995, Ramsey 1997, Handler 1988, Wulff 2003 and 2007).

5. In September 1958, Guinea voted 'No' to the constitution proposed by de Gaulle's government which aimed to change the relationship of France to the Union of French West Africa. Thus Guinea became the first country of the union to gain independence (Johnson 1978: 37).

6. Dancers as 'cultural ambassadors' are not specific to West Africa. The management of the UK's Royal Ballet promoted this same approach (Wulff 2002: 67).

7. Guinea's poor economy is the result, among others, of France's under-investment during colonialism, the country's government mismanagement and corruption as well as Touré's 'erratic' foreign policy which led to the alienation of Guinea from its neighbours and the international community (Harshe 1984, Johnson 1978).

8. Population movements within the region preceded and continued during colonialism (Ndiaye 2008: 409). According to the World Bank Migration and Remittances Factbook 2011, Senegal is the second destination for Guinean migrants after Côte d'Ivoire (retrieved 13 September 2012). IOM's National Profile for Senegal (2009) indicates that Guinean migrants are the majority migrant population, representing 39 per cent of the

total immigrant population of Senegal (IOM 2009: 25). In the past, Guineans worked in the groundnut agriculture in Senegal, fought as part of the French army at the end of the nineteenth century (Diallo 2009: 26) and migrated to Senegal in large numbers following the independence of Guinea and Senegal and into the 1970s (ibid.: 11), in part out of disagreement with Touré's regime (ibid.: 41).

9. During this fieldwork, Senegal mediated again between Guinea and the world in February 2007. Guinea experienced social unrest as workers' unions went on strike in protest against the president at that time, Conté (see Lydia Polgreen, 'Discontent in Guinea Nears Boiling Point', *New York Times*, 20 February 2007). As a result international organizations relocated their staff temporarily to Senegal and similarly U.S. students of West African dance moved to Dakar, at times along with their Guinean teachers.

10. Interestingly, there is no ballet in Senegal with an exclusively Sabar repertoire. When Sabar is included in a performance it takes no more than twenty minutes of a performance that may last for over an hour (Masamba Gueye, Dakar, 2007). Many Senegalese claim that Djembé is superior on the grounds that it comes from a 'richer tradition'. This may be a reflection of the consistently bigger international market for Djembé. Teachers' reasons for the sustained popularity of Djembé in New York included: that it is exported by many countries (Mali, Guinea, Ghana, Nigeria, etc.) in contrast to Sabar that is specific to Senegal and The Gambia; that Djembé has a bigger market for students and thus Senegalese dancers prefer to teach Djembé over Sabar; that Djembé simply 'got to the States first' in contrast to Sabar, which arrived there in the late 1980s; that students are more familiar with Djembé because the first Senegalese teachers were perhaps not competent or confident to teach Sabar; and that Djembé is simply easier and thus more accessible to a larger audience.

11. Katherine Dunham was also the first to conduct anthropological fieldwork on dance in Haiti in the 1930s. According to Ramsey, Dunham's position as an African American female led her to depart from her initial agenda influenced by her supervisor, Herskovits, who viewed the Caribbean as an ideal research site to study the retention of African elements and to decipher a 'scale of intensity of Africanisms' (Ramsey 2000: 201). Dunham continued to work as a dancer and a choreographer, developed the Dunham technique and popularized dances from the Diaspora.

12. On Diaspora dances, see Browning 1995, Daniel 1995, Dobbin 1986, Drewal 1989, Dunham 1969, Hazzard-Gordon 1990, Walker 2001.

13. Senegalese emigration rose in the 1980s as a result of Structural Adjustment Programs (SAPs) implemented in 1981 that impacted negatively on social welfare and increased poverty (Lopez and Hathie 1998; see also Coulon and Cruise O'Brien 1989: 156–57 for a concise overview of Senegal's finances up to the SAPs). New York became a destination for Senegalese migrants partly due to the decreasing opportunities to previously popular destinations such as France, and a new direct flight from Dakar to New York (Perry 1997). For the religious organization of New York's Senegalese migrants, see Malcomson (1996), Ba (2008), Babou (2002). See also Stoller (2002) on migrants from Niger and Mali working in the informal New York economy.

14. Interview with the author, New York, 2006.

15. 'Cultural capital' is a term introduced by Bourdieu to explain how symbolic violence – 'the imposition of a cultural arbitrary by an arbitrary power' (1977: 5) – is exercised in

class systems (Bourdieu and Passeron 1977: 30). In this book cultural capital refers to the 'cultural goods', the knowledge West African artists possess and – being aware of its value – are able to commodify accordingly.

16. In the Sahel, slaves were outsiders to the societies in which they were brought in as captives, or through trade. In some cases, the second generation merged through marriage into the lineages of the noble families for whom the slaves worked (Meillasoux 1991). In Senegambia, Searing argues that generational and occupational differences lead to great distinctions of status within the slave population, with 'household slaves' having rights to the use of land, 'and rights to substitute tribute payments for labor services' (Searing 1988: 480).

17. Lamine was drawn to dancing as a kid because of the American pop stars Michael Jackson and MC Hammer. He used to enter break dancing competitions hosted by nightclubs that awarded prizes. Following continual success, Lamine was encouraged to dance professionally.

18. Neveu Kringelbach (2005) provides an insightful account of the politics, promises and disappointments involved in pursuing a career as a ballet dancer. Other than the money, dancers are attracted by the status inferred by the act of travelling. The opportunities to travel, however, are negotiated between the members of ballet companies, a negotiation in which certain personal qualities, one's gender or educational level, work to disadvantage some dancers.

19. This is common throughout West Africa as specialists like sorcerers and weavers believe their particular skill comes from blood as well as from the ingestion of medicines that enhance drumming, weaving, or magical power (see Stoller and Olkes 1987, Stoller 2004, Chernoff 1979).

20. Tang argues that '"it's in my blood" reflects a matrilineal inheritance' (Diop 1981: 20 in Tang 2007: 58).

21. 'Culture' here denotes his *géwël* background, consistent with Dilley's argument that race, culture and ethnicity are notions of alterity comparable to that of 'caste' (2000).

22. It is worth pointing out that professional dancers who train and perform in the Euro-American dance tradition and those performing in traditional and folkloric ballets abide by the Euro-American aesthetic.

23. *Tour* is used to refer to a wide range of events but generally involves a specific group of people who take turns in organizing them (Neveu Kringelbach 2005). *Tours* are organized for the purpose of entertainment and allow participants to maintain contact with friends and family. As the participants contribute financially to the event the hostess is able to raise a small amount of money for her private use (ibid.). See Neveu Kringelbach (2005) for an insightful analysis of the economic structure of Senegalese women's associations and of gender relations in Sabar.

24. For a detailed account of the organization of different Sabars from the perspective of drummers, see Tang (2007).

25. The gender imbalance in New York is partly due to traditional ideas about gender, 'caste' and dance which discouraged female dancers from entering dance troupes and from migrating (see Neveu Kringelbach 2005: 63). However, this is a trend that is changing as female dancers join Senegalese women from other professions in international migration (Neveu Kringelbach 2005, Ba 2008, Babou 2008).

Chapter 2

The New York Dance Floor

Edited Field Notes, New York, 24 September 2006
'I hope she is not too late today' someone says. West African dance teachers are notorious for being late and Aminata is not expected to differ. I rush to change and then into the studio. The YMCA on 14th Street is strikingly different from the one in Harlem. Newly painted and very clean, it even provides fresh towels. The room is packed with colourful outfits: traditional Senegalese clothes of matching tops and skirts made out of wax fabrics, with beaded *bechos* under their skirts.[1] Everyone seems to adhere to the international dress for West African classes, with just a bit of extra attentiveness this time for the special occasion. Aminata walks in thirty minutes late, very confident, very loud and very funny. The studio is rather small and there are about fifty of us – two men and the rest women. In the imperative, the favourite form in Wolof, Aminata goes step by step through a choreography of Kaolack: 'OK, this is the step! One, two, jump, one, two, three, jump. Do it again! Go!' The sequence is choreographed so that it is easy to remember. Movements are repeated with slight variations. We go over the choreography many times, half the class clapping the rhythm while the other half dances. Aminata sings the introduction to guide us when to start. She encourages us to dance energetically: 'Come on! Give it to me hard!', triggering a burst of laughter. We complete the choreography, the drummers enter the room, they take their places and the drumming begins. For the rest of the class Aminata shows us different moves to imitate. The movements are very different from what we have so far been taught by our male teachers. At the end of the class we

form a circle and one by one enter to dance. 'Excuse me! Excuse me!', Aminata interrupts the drumming, 'No more drama please! We don't need any drama and that Uptown-Downtown, that's bullshit!' Someone calls, 'Yeah, say it sister!' 'Excuse me! Excuse me! African dance is about happiness. It should all be about happiness!' Someone interrupts her in support again. 'You agree with me but let me finish! If we come with evil in our mind, we won't be able to dance. We need to have a clear mind to dance!' Cheering and applause cover her voice. Allah is mentioned, the phrase 'drummers yo!' and it all ends with another burst of laughter. As we approach the end of the class Aminata announces the host teacher's birthday and the entire class sings Stevie Wonder's 1980s 'Happy Birthday'.[2]

I had just started fieldwork and Aminata's 'Uptown-Downtown' speech seemed cryptic. Nothing had happened in class – nothing that you could see – to trigger her sermon. The Uptown-Downtown tension however underlines many New York West African classes, and expresses a tension between the different understandings of those involved in the classes. Geographical tensions between New York boroughs and neighbourhoods is a more general attitude amongst New Yorkers who will for example not venture from the Upper West Side to the Upper East Side or from Queens to Brooklyn. In the case of West African dances however, Uptown and Downtown also denote different groups of participants, different reasons for engaging with the dances and consequently different types of West African dance. The tension between Uptown and Downtown here is about authority and appropriation and about contested attempts by different actors to define what the classes are about.

Here I approach New York City Sabar classes in line with Cowan's conception of a dance-event as a 'temporally, spatially, and conceptually "bounded" sphere of interaction' (Cowan 1990: 4), a site where meanings are negotiated. Cowan explored dance-events in northern Greece as sites for the negotiation of meanings in relation to the gendered body, arguing that gender inequalities produce an inequality of power amongst competing voices that allow some understandings to persist over others (1990). The power of the different voices, however, is not static but shifting, as for example a woman's power changes according to her social status, married women being more powerful than unmarried ones. Similarly, Sabar classes in New York provide the grounds for the negotiation of different meanings, as participants manipulate space and time to introduce different hierarchies and locate themselves in them. These hierarchies are made on the grounds of dancing skills and commitment to the dance forms, as well as on the grounds of affinity to the forms. In creating these hierarchies dancers claim their 'place' in the class in relation to others and define the events. Their power to do so, however, is also shifting as they compete with hierarchies

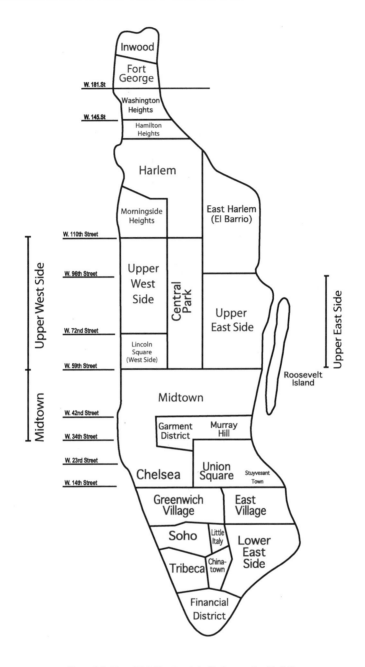

Figure 2.1 Map of Neighbourhoods in Manhattan, New York City
Map designed by Aurélie Mertenat for the purpose of this publication

introduced by other dancers. In the following sections I delineate the different spaces where West African dance forms Sabar and Djembé are found and the understandings of the participants involved. I explore the ways in which these different voices are negotiated on the dance floor in distinctly bodily ways and how the forms change by moving through the different performance spaces.

In Manhattan there are two geographic areas that offer two different types of West African dance classes. 'Downtown' classes (from 14th to 59th Street) are paid for, teachers are West African migrants and students come from diverse backgrounds (African American, European American and Asian American, as well as other internationals). 'Uptown' classes (from 114th to 144th Street, in Harlem) are free, and teachers and students are primarily from African American and West Indian backgrounds (see Fig. 2.1). As implied in the demographics of the participants, the distinction between Uptown and Downtown classes is not merely a geographical one. Downtown classes take place in studios that host different dance and acting classes. The YMCA on 135th Street in Harlem also serves as a space where Djembé and Sabar classes are taught for a fee, and so does the Alvin Ailey American Dance Theatre that held a beginners' Sabar class in 2006. West African dances are also taught for a fee throughout the year in camps, workshops and conferences around the United States.

Sabar classes in New York are almost exclusively taught by Senegalese Downtown, while Djembé classes are taught primarily by Guinean dancers and African American teachers Uptown. During this fieldwork (summers of 2006 and 2008) there were three male dancers holding regular weekly Sabar classes in Manhattan. Other dancers taught occasionally in workshops or as substitute teachers who visited New York from around the States. 'Uptown', in Harlem, there is at least one 'African' dance class every day of the working week, taught by African American or West Indian dancers. The majority of participants are also from an African American or West Indian background. At the time of this research there were four teachers holding regular classes, the majority of whom were female. Uptown classes are generally referred to as 'community' classes. They are held in high school gymnasiums and government-funded buildings and are free for the students.

Downtown's Move! Dance Center

Edited Field Notes, New York, 26 July 2006
I walk out of the subway and into New York's summer heat. Walking towards the studio I hear the drumming from the street. Move! Dance Center is conveniently accessible via many subway lines and has a long history of monopolizing 'exotic' dance classes: from belly dancing to Capoeira, Djembé and Sabar, Congolese, Afro-Cuban, Afro-Haitian, Mambo, Salsa and Samba. In the past, Move! has featured in the local media as the best dance studio of its kind. Move! is very popular. The

owner appears in advertisements as a self-made, hard-working man, while notorious amongst participants for being profit driven at the expense of clients and teachers. The standard fee in New York City is $15.00 for ninety minutes of class. You can save one dollar per class by paying for a block of ten. Move! offers deals where one can earn free classes. True to the proclaimed 'serious business approach' of the owner, the conditions for these schemes make them nearly impossible to get. The studios are badly maintained and poorly air-conditioned; the dressing rooms cramped and seemingly unhygienic. Dance teachers are said to get less than 50 per cent of what their students' pay, while substitute teachers are paid even less. Rumour has it that the owner is even less generous with the newly arrived migrants and U.S. volunteers. In the owner's defence, the stable existence of the studio guarantees an income for the recently arrived artists who are unfamiliar to students. The studio advertises the classes and manages the schedule, a notably weak area for the newly arrived teachers who often rely on friends and partners for this. Move! also allows drumming, which is rare in New York where studio space is limited and thus there is a risk of neighbours' complaints. All of the above make Move! a unique studio where classes are offered by both older and newly arrived teachers.

I enter the building and a student complains about the heat and the deteriorating condition of the building. The elevator is broken so we take the stairs. At the reception I overhear more complaints, this time about a dance teacher who has been teaching 'modern Haitian' while the student wants 'traditional stuff'. I move towards the dressing room and find a room packed with sweating bodies trying to manoeuvre into clean clothes. Very few choose to shower there as the showers seem to malfunction as a reminder of the studio's poor maintenance. I change next to two women, both advanced students. They discuss a Djembé retreat organized for the following weekend by Youssouf Koumbassa, one of the most proclaimed Guinean Djembé teachers in New York. Her friend complains about the previous night's Sabar class: 'People try to show off rather than learn!' I leave the studio and a sign tells me not to blame Move! for any injuries and to dance at my own risk. Outside the class another sign forbids photographing and videotaping. I take my place on the floor and wait for the teacher. The above summarizes the main themes of Downtown classes. They are part of a business-like environment: recognized as profitable and marketed accordingly. The studios are conveniently located in Lower Manhattan and are thus easily accessible. The teachers are usually from West Africa and the Caribbean, and the classes create an all-inclusive environment by accommodating an ethnically mixed group of students.

In choosing to attend a Downtown class one is choosing to learn Djembé or Sabar from the 'source'. To a certain extent, most West African dancers have a similar 'cultural capital'. They are often *griot* and thus posses the knowledge of their respective traditions. Furthermore, many of them have had similar training in performing in traditional ballets. Most dancers also employ similar pedagogical techniques as older teachers introduce newcomers to what U.S. students prefer. This means that the competition between dancers is different in nature than one might imagine. Dancers promote themselves through their background (as *griot* or as professional dancers in ballets) but not necessarily in comparison to others. Students' preference for one teacher over another depends on many things, like the teacher's style as well as the demographic make-up and energy of the class and the degree of convenience of its time and location. Teachers' dancing and teaching styles often determine who their students are and consequently affect the class atmosphere. Among teachers, style is discussed as innate rather than acquired, and so I was never present at conversations where envy was expressed on the grounds of style. Envy however was expressed for a teacher's 'following' – that is, regular students – as this meant a stable income. Other than a teacher's style, the ability to maintain a following depended on how committed they were to holding weekly classes. Those who did not hold regular classes were aware that it is 'bad for business' as students 'forget you'. They seemed to do so however out of choice; as one dancer explained, he preferred to teach workshops around the U.S. than to remain in one place. Regardless, since there are relatively few Sabar teachers in New York, new teachers are seen as an opportunity to develop one's practice.

Politics on the Dance Floor

The Structure of West African Dance Classes

Djembé and Sabar classes in New York have the same general structure. Depending on the preference of the teacher, time will be allocated differently between the different parts. The class begins with a 5–30 minute warm up, which may include stretching, push-ups, sit-ups, as well as movements that students find difficult, the idea being that with repetition students will learn them. For the majority of class time, instructors teach one to three short choreographies of a Sabar dance-rhythm. Teachers introduce the dance by giving the name of the rhythm and some background information on the area or country of origin and/ or the occasion of the performance. The choreography is taught one movement at a time, and at the end the full choreography is performed to drumming. In the next part of the class the students go across the floor in lines of two to four per line, one line behind another. The instructor demonstrates a short sequence of movements and each line of dancers repeats the sequence while advancing to the other side of the class, thus allowing the next line to follow behind them. The drummers usually sit on the opposite side of the room so that dancers face them while advancing. The advanced students go in the front lines, followed by the intermediate and finally the beginners. The few men in the class form the last line. While simple in theory, forming lines is very political as will be discussed below. Depending on the teacher, the type of class and the remaining time, a class may end with the 'circle'. Community classes in Harlem almost always end with a circle, but in commercial studios it is not very common. Participants encircle a space in front of the drummers and whoever wishes to can enter the circle to perform a short solo. This is the time when students show off their skills and their appreciation for the class.

André's Class, Edited Field Notes, 6 September 2006
André has been teaching Sabar in New York for over a decade. A former member of one of the biggest Senegalese ballets, André was introduced into the New York Sabar scene as a substitute teacher. He was soon offered his own weekly class and has held regular classes ever since. André has a very committed following of students, some of whom rarely attend classes taught by others. Compared to other West African teachers who are notorious for not starting class on time, André is reliable. He is never late and always makes sure to arrange a substitute teacher for when he is away. The class is full of colourful skirts, *lapas*, and matching shirts. This international uniform for West African dance classes takes many forms in the different body shapes and colour combinations. The students are mostly women and, like most downtown classes, the ethnic make-up is mixed. André is concerned with teaching us proper technique. He insists on endless repetitions and interrupts the class when he is not satisfied. The students encourage this. The best students move to the front of the class and provide examples for the others to follow.

The class begins when André connects his iPod to the speakers and the room fills with music: a Mbalax version of Stevie Wonder's 'Pastime Paradise' in Wolof lyrics. André begins his warm-up routine and we follow his silent instruction. We stretch our legs then slowly rotate our heads . . . The class is only half full, but not for long. Women move in and out of the dressing rooms, greet each other loudly in the hallways and peek through the door, calculating when to join. Many will enter the class after the warm-up. Some of them will move quietly to the back of the class and others to the front, silently establishing their 'place' in the class. 'That was a great warm-up André! The best one you've ever done!' says one of the latecomers. 'Yeah . . . you only caught about a minute of it!' he replies, as the whole class bursts out in laughter. This exact teasing routine was repeated in last Saturday's class. It comes from one of André's committed students, whose late entrance and open affinity with André marks 'her place' in the class.

Line Formation: Space and Time

Negotiating space and time in class is a way to establish one's presence and at the same time define the purpose of the class. Throughout the class, students reproduce teachers' movements. There is a specific sequence to follow in the warm-up, a specific choreography in the main part of the class and the same movements to imitate when 'going across the floor'. This encourages dancers into homogeneity, as they must move through time and space in unison. However, dancers will show off their abilities by 'playing' with the limits of the movements, allowing more space for their own style and thus promoting themselves as good dancers. The very ability to negotiate time and space on the dance floor is indicative of one's 'place' in the class, one's abilities as a dancer and one's relations to others. Negotiating space creates hierarchies and marking one's place can be done for different reasons, at an individual or group level.

Downtown Divas

When it is time to form lines, the drummers enter the studio and the dancers move to the side. The class will be shown a short sequence, and then imitate it in lines of three. While simple in theory, forming lines is very subtle and political. In the first line stand the advanced dancers who are able to 'catch' movements and imitate them instantly, irrespective of difficulty. Others rarely take the responsibility and chance to go first. What happens with the rest of the lines is that people approach the spots they would like to take while making eye contact with those who they want to join them. Encouraging nods from the teacher and others signal 'go ahead', while avoiding eye contact, no nodding or discouraging expressions show others' disagreement. One's decision of which line to join depends on how good one thinks one is, and how good others, and at times the instructor, think one is. As the line reflects back on one's own dancing abilities, one prefers to be in a line with equally good or better dancers. At the same time, as the dancers of each line move together, the line looks better when all members are of comparable skill. If dancers end up in a line with someone they have not chosen, they can exclude them by not coordinating with them.

However, one's dancing abilities can also be negotiated, thus changing one's place in the lines. Dancers with weak technique may employ an 'attitude' of confidence to negotiate their skills. Instead of imitating the movements shown by the teacher, they may substitute these with similar movements they already know.

> I see a lot of girls dancing very well, better than me, but they are not observing because what they do is completely different from what he's doing! They look very confident, they change the move completely, and you have the feeling that they are the best, like the one that's standing at

the end . . . Fantastic! It's a joy to see it! But she's not doing what he's doing! (Stella, New York, 2008)

Some teachers will call on this and correct it but most often it will go unchallenged. This 'attitude' has an effect on newcomers who generally accept it and translate it as advanced dancing skills. Advanced students, however, will be more critical and harder to persuade. As Claire explains:

I found it really intimidating in the beginning. Like many women even in their attitude and when I was new I was not able to see this well . . . Now that I've sort of seen more, I'm like 'OK, you might be on the front line and have that attitude' but now I see there's people who don't progress . . . they do the things they've always done, and you know, intimidate newcomers I guess. (Claire, New York, 2008)

Other than using one's dancing to negotiate dancing abilities, time can be employed to the same end. By not conforming to the same timeline as others, one can declare a unique standing in the class and draw attention to oneself and one's line. In that case, dancers will 'hold' their line and not start when they are supposed to. They will interrupt the regular flow of lines and thus draw more attention to their line:

Yup! There's always the stand off of all the 'divas' that always have to go at the end and . . . there always seems to be this huge gap for like the last three lines . . . They all seem to just slowly form together and they'll make sure they are exactly with who they want to be and the other lines end up being almost across the floor before they go . . . I've found [them] to be the most intimidating and if you notice they'll never take chances of going on the front line and I find it interesting. (Claire, New York, 2008)

In this case, space and time are employed by some to promote themselves as good dancers. These dancers are often disapprovingly referred to as 'divas', implying that their defining characteristic is their 'diva' attitude and not their dancing abilities. This breeds a competitive atmosphere that not all students enjoy. Space and time here are negotiated to create a hierarchy amongst dancers defined on the basis of dancing, albeit performed, abilities and technique. Space and time, however, can also be negotiated to define a class-event at a group level.

Community and the Others

You know, I mean honestly, before I came to New York, I don't think I ever took an African class with anyone white in there! Only when I came here, which wasn't a big deal to me but to some people that's a big deal. Now, some people are concerned if you gotta go take class Downtown, the make-up . . . the composition of the student body is very mixed, and just with a whole different subject. Because of that it doesn't bring that sense of community, that sense of connection you know, and a lot of people don't like it! (Nicole, New York, 2008)

Nicole explains how the mixed environment of African American and 'Other' students in Downtown classes keeps Uptown participants away. In African American vernacular dances in the 1900s, Hazzard-Gordon (1985) explains that outsiders' attendance was seen as an 'intrusion': 'This response is a group sensitivity that reflects the almost territorial guardianship with which most blacks, even those incapable of dancing, view the dance' (1985: 440). The attempt to define the classes as a 'community' affair is expressed Downtown in the way lines are formed, as some students create exclusively African American lines. This does not define everyone's actions, and rarely happens amongst long-standing participants of the classes or amongst participants who know each other personally. This is consistent with Orbe and Harris (2008) that interracial communication in America is placed along an 'interpersonal/intergroup continuum'; that is, if people are familiar with each other, then race is not important.[3] As I discuss below, this attitude also depends on the teacher.

This community feeling is also expressed in the way the lines are formed in class. Thus, as a non-African American you may be avoided by African Americans who will either not step up to fill the spots next to you or may give you a discouraging look if you step up to join their line. If someone initiates a non-African American line they may also be eagerly joined by others who want to avoid the discomfort of being rejected from an African American line. Line formation is so subtle that it rarely becomes obvious to newcomers or to those observing the class. For example an apprentice drummer in the class confessed his surprise when informed of this practice by a student. One of the few times exclusion was expressed through means other than negotiating space was in the final part of the class, during the students' solo performances in a circle. On one occasion a Japanese student performed a solo that received rousing applause from many of us, including the Senegalese teacher and a Senegalese dancer attending the class. The sentiment however was not shared by some of the African American students present who refused to applaud and thus to recognize the quality of the dancing. Not everyone attempts to define a class as a community affair, and those who position themselves within different hierarchies often openly resist it, as will be discussed below.

Above I discussed how by negotiating space and time one can establish one's position as a dancer within the hierarchy of the class or define the events at the group level. These strategies are used to claim a more powerful voice over others and to define the purpose of the class. This resonates with Ardener's 'muted group' theory (1975) that different groups hold different views of 'reality'. The 'reality' of the group with the more powerful voice becomes the dominant one while other voices are muted, never becoming part of the dominant discourse. Here, the power of the different voices is expressed in uniquely bodily terms, by negotiating space and time. Furthermore, 'muteness' is not a permanent condition but always relational, with different groups slipping in and out of 'muteness' in relation to others. In this case, African American participants, a historically 'mute group' in the U.S. (Orbe 1995), 'mute' non-African American participants by negotiating the time and space on the dance floor to form the 'dominant discourse' within the events. In the following section I will explore in detail what the negotiated meanings are – that is, what it means for both Uptown community participants as well as the Downtown non-African American participants to engage with West African dances. In the final part of the chapter I will discuss the views of African American and other participants who resist both of the above-mentioned hierarchies and attempts to define the classes, and instead introduce a third hierarchy, on the grounds of a serious commitment to the dances.

Community Classes

'African dance' classes in Harlem take place in public buildings and recreational centres.[4] They are free as they are funded by the Beacon Program, put into effect in 1991 by the first African American Mayor of New York City David N. Dinkins, later supported by Mayor Giuliani as a 'crime prevention measure' (Krauss 1994). The policy design intention is to engage children in after-school activities like sports, arts, tutoring and job training sessions. 'African dance' classes are attended by adult women and, at times, their children. The Beacon Program provides a standard salary for the teacher, but teachers also hold day-time jobs. Questioners at the entrance of each class monitor attendance and participants' demographics. Many students neglect the attendance sheet, which is a problem for teachers as attendance is important in securing future funding for the continuation of the classes. In the summers of 2006 and 2008 there were free classes every day of the week. All teachers were female and African American with the exception of one male dancer and one second-generation female dancer from the West Indies. Uptown students were primarily from an African American background and almost exclusively female, with no more than eight men in a fifty-student class. As there are different movements for men and women in West African dances, men only attend if the teacher can teach 'male' movements. Classes are listed as 'African dance' or 'West African dance' and primarily teach Djembé. Participants refer to Harlem classes as 'community' classes, which are seen as a primarily African American affair.[5] Most teachers came to African dances having trained in other dance forms. Vicky for example explained that she faced obstacles in her professional dance career because her body did not fit the aesthetics of ballet at the time: 'Your legs are too thick, your body is too long, your muscles are too dense'.[6] In contrast, Marie had no previous experience with other dances and was only drawn to African dances. Teachers' different trajectories are reflected in their classes.

Vicky's Class, Edited Field Notes, 25 July 2006
I am heading to a class on 125th Street. I've been told that Vicky has 'great energy' and I'm eager to discover why but I cannot find the entrance to the building. It is hot and humid in New York and the streets are full of kids running through the spraying water of fire hydrants. Older people are sitting chatting on their stoops. I decide to approach one for directions. He points me to the gate across the street where I find a sign-in sheet and fill in my ethnicity, level of education, income and home address. There are posters on the walls: the seven principles of Kwanzaa and a quote by Michael Jordan: 'just play, have fun, enjoy the game'.[7] Other than spreading their moral intentions, these posters address themes relevant to the African American audience that moves through these spaces.

I enter the dressing rooms, vibrant from women cracking jokes and exchanging greetings. Some complain they haven't seen each other for a while. Others exchange notes on Downtown classes and newly arrived teachers from West Africa. The friendly, jovial atmosphere is punctuated by unexpected remarks:
- . . . calluses drop right off your feet! It's better than a razor 'cos you don't have to do anything!
- and what does it do to the rest of your skin? Oh, I'm scaaared! Takes the calluses right off! What kinda chemical is that? That must be some pooootent shit!

This friendly atmosphere carries into the class, the High School's basketball court. Amongst the primarily African American female students there are four men, a few children, two international students and myself. Vicky announces the dance of the day and teaches us the accompanying song. It is a Malinke dance from Guinea and we sing a 'call and response' sequence in Swahili.

Mixing aspects from different ethnic traditions, in this case an East African language with a West African dance, is common in these classes where Africa is conceived and produced as one entity. As Stoller writes:

The search for cultural meaning and personal meaningful-ness in Afrocentrism is centered on the reduplication of a monolithic Africa that, in turn, reinforces communal principles in Africa America. The ideal Africa articulated in Afrocentric signs is one in which to paraphrase Baudrillard, nostalgia is energized, in which 'there is a proliferation of myths of origin and signs of reality'. In Afrocentrism, African values, mores, and ideas, do not come from an Africa of the recent past; rather they have their origin in distant times. (Stoller 2002: 85)[8]

The Afrocentric approach defines these classes as a uniquely 'African' affair. As Gilroy (1993: 263) and Clifford (1997) argue, the 'mixing' of different, seemingly contradictory elements and practices is a characteristic of Diaspora cultures who 'work to maintain community, selectively preserving and recovering traditions, "customizing" and "revisioning" them in novel, hybrid, and often antagonistic situations' (Clifford 1997: 258).

The general feeling of a 'community' class however is not educational but fun. This is evident in the women's dancing, the singing along and the teasing. 'Fun' is for some participants the fundamental characteristic of community classes:

Whereas we have a variety of people who come and can't execute the movements that well, they come for fun! And even though you know I do some technical stuff sometimes, I want people to have fun first and foremost – it's about fun, dance should be fun! (Marie, New York, 2006)

I remember one class . . . the back couple of rows would be good . . . they were dancers, probably people who danced in companies and all. Everyone else was just there to enjoy themselves. (Michelle, New York, 2008)

For Michelle, this fun environment is encouraged by the fact that the classes are free:

Uptown classes have a whole different mentality going on for multiple reasons. I found there was a much greater sense of community . . . its not really about . . . its about dance but its about enjoying your time with these people, with that teacher, with the drummers, the drummers all come and volunteer for free . . . that mentality is supported by the fact that it's a free class, and I think if they had to pay for it they would have a different perspective on it. So it makes it easy for the people to come and socialize. (Michelle, New York, 2008)

Thus 'community' classes are primarily about enjoying oneself, asserting a community feeling and one's belonging to that community.[9] The sense of community is activated in many ways, such as community announcements at the end of each class or by evoking common, past experiences. For example Vicky showed us a move, and called out 'Hammertime!' to help us to understand it. The room was instantly filled with women's complaints; the move was too difficult. Some students refused to participate and instead started joking: 'You do it, we'll call "Hammertime!"' An Asian American student asked what 'Hammertime' meant and a student explained the reference to the 1990s African American pop star MC Hammer. To an outsider, such instances reflect unfamiliarity with the shared past experiences and knowledge of the participants of community classes. The same elements that mark this class as a common experience for some also mark the exclusion of others, like myself, who may be present but are outsiders to the shared knowledge of the participants.

'Community' is given continuity through the participation of children and older members. The history of the community was for example pronounced in the birthday celebration of one of the older members, Mrs Jones. We celebrated Mrs Jones's birthday in three different community classes with different teachers. The celebration took place at the end of each class, when a magnificent, colourful cake was wheeled in and shared with the participants. Women and children performed solos in the circle to honour Mrs Jones. We sang Stevie Wonder's 'Happy Birthday', and participants shared stories of Mrs Jones's life and involvement in New York City's African dance scene. 'Community' is also given continuity through the children. Some mothers may bring their children to class for 'functional reasons', for example to avoid arranging for babysitters. Classes are also educational, as in Vicky's words: 'kids learn the culture in their hearts and in their brains through these classes'. Whatever the reasons, the presence of the younger members reinforces the sense of community.

Finally, the community feeling becomes most explicit through the use of kinship terminology. Terms like *our elders, our ancestors, sisters, brothers* and *family* create kinship between participants, reinforcing the community feeling while also excluding those who do not 'fit' the category. Kinship terminology thus has the same effect as shared experiences which, when evoked, define participants in relation to their belonging to 'the community'. For Hazzard-Gordon, dance has historically been an important arena for African Americans to establish a feeling of belonging, as dance reinforces 'cultural identity':

Dance becomes a litmus test for cultural identity. Proper Afro-American dance demands the demonstration of certain postures and gestures held in esteem in black culture; through the dance, one proves that one is a member of the cultural body, that one is truly in touch with the cultural material. (Hazzard-Gordon 1985: 431)

The dances carry with them an implied context of socio-cultural experience. They help to define one as a black person, but especially as a black person who has not been removed from one's people and cultural roots. (Ibid.: 434)[10]

While proving 'blackness' through dance was initially an aspect of working-class African Americans, Hazzard-Gordon argues that it penetrated through other social strata in the 1960s to include even the 'black elite' (ibid.). Hazzard-Gordon's discussion focuses on an earlier period of African American vernacular dance and not on 'African dances' per se; however, her analysis reinforces the sense of belonging that dance holds for African American participants. Establishing one's belonging is a characteristic of Diaspora discourse that as Clifford says 'articulates, or bends roots *and* routes to construct what Gilroy (1986) describes as alternate public spheres, forms of community consciousness and solidarity that maintain identifications outside the national time/space in order to live inside, with difference' (Clifford 1997: 251). Building further on Gilroy (1993), Clifford continues that 'the term "diaspora" is a signifier not simply of transnationality and movement but of political struggles to define the local, as distinctive community, in historical contexts of displacement' (Clifford 1997: 252).[11] Belonging is an important aspect of 'community' classes.

Traditionalists vs. Innovators

All of the above elements make Vicky's class familiar and fun; a 'community' affair. Harlem classes are preferred for their community feeling but not all teachers prescribe to the community agenda. Some African American teachers actively distance themselves. This however is often met with criticism from the 'traditionalists'. Aisha and Issa are two such examples as they have unique approaches to the teaching of West African dance. For Issa, like many others, the value of West African dance technique remains widely unacknowledged. They argue that in the U.S., African dance is still seen as the simple shaking of one's body. Issa, like other dancers, see it as their responsibility to change this perception.[12] To this end, Issa structures his classes differently from community classes by dedicating more time to teaching technique.

Issa's Class, Edited Field Notes, 18 July 2006
Issa interrupts our dancing: 'There's the people from the village . . . This ain't the village, we didn't just get the drums out playing and dancing how we feel [he mockingly imitates stereotypical 'African' moves] . . . 'I'm not saying that anyone here is from the village . . . but the reason we have been doing this choreography for so long is so that you can do it well.'

For Issa, 'community' classes do not always promote an appreciation of the dances' technique, a point which he chooses to address in his classes: 'I try to discourage the community aspect of it because I think that exists in enough other African dance classes. That doesn't need to be the purpose of my class. I try to make the purpose of my class noting the work. That doesn't mean that I negate the other experiences . . . I've done that, conducted it, but when you turn up in this class, I want you to walk out with some kind of understanding of what I'm trying to teach'.

Issa introduces every dance with a rich background on its origins in an attempt to embed them in a social and historical context. The dances are not simply a technique, and so after the warm-up Issa turns to face the class and to narrate the relevant information on the dances. This positioning reinforces the class's educational intent. Issa's style derives from a constantly evolving understanding of his positioning as an African American who, born through the Black Power movement into Afrocentricity, later embraced his self-acceptance as someone who embodies elements of what he calls his 'African American reality'. This personal experience shapes the narratives and aesthetics of his choreographies, which he describes as a 'Neo-African' aesthetic and links to pan-Africanism. This aesthetic is expressed in his teaching where he uses 'traditional' movements as the basis for his choreographies.

Aisha is another teacher who builds a unique agenda on West African dance. For Aisha dancing has great healing powers and she employs what she calls 'creative visualization' to help her students. At the beginning of the class, students meditate with their eyes closed and work through breathing exercises. Aisha encourages them to imagine a bright glow with healing powers in different parts of their bodies. She uses positive affirmations to encourage her students' sense of empowerment: 'I'm a healthy, beautiful, wonderful woman, and I deserve the best and the best will happen'. Aisha chooses a different dance every time to relate her teachings and the purpose of each class to current events. For example to commemorate the victims of 9/11 on 11 September 2006, Lamban was chosen as a dance for the ancestors.[13] The day triggered Aisha's own thoughts on war, life and death, and her suggestions for a successful approach to life. For Aisha, a class is an occasion to share values that she believes can help everyone to live better; and West African dances can also accommodate 'other beliefs'. She thus fuses the dances with Eastern philosophy and Buddhist meditation techniques, which she uses to reflect on current events and social issues. For Aisha, West African dances are an expression of a more humane existence and can lead to a more peaceful life.

Thus Uptown classes can vary greatly in intent. While for the majority they are seen as 'community' affairs, teachers can also incorporate their own agendas in the teaching of traditional dances. This however exposes other tensions that highlight the importance of the notion of community for some participants. Some argue that 'African dance' should be guided by respect for tradition and thus see approaches like Issa's and Aisha's as non-traditional, which Aisha acknowledged: 'Sometimes people who are traditionalists are not too happy about the traditions being innovated on. They feel that you'll lose a bit of what our ancestors left behind – and it's understandable.' Traditionalists want to maintain a connection to the past and the ancestors. Dance can offer this connection as long as it is performed 'traditionally'. Dance is treated as static and non-evolving, thus representing while also allowing a connection between the present and the past, and between Africa and America:

> in the diaspora experience, the co-presence of 'here' and 'there' is articulated in antiteleological (sometimes messianic) temporality. Linear history is broken, the present constantly shadowed by a past that is also a desired, but obstructed, future: a renewed, painful yearning . . . Afrocentric attempts to evoke a direct connection with Africa, often bypassing this constitutive predicament, are both escapist and ahistorical. (Clifford 1997: 264)

This, for Aisha, is a problem unique to African Americans that people from the West Indies who share similar 'dance roots' do not have. Aisha believes that by naming dances as Afro-Cuban or Afro-Haitian they have acknowledged the past and also allowed innovation.

For Issa, a concern with tradition is not necessarily an attachment to the past but instead to present-day Africa and Africans:[14]

> The African Americans were trying to stick to the traditional cause; it was all about trying to be as Africans as we can be . . . there's some people who are still caught up in that, but they are people who are the old heads, you know, conformists. (Issa, New York, 2006)

Traditionalists also resonate with those concerned with originality and 'authenticity':

> or you find the young people, who like anything, when they start learning something they become passionate about it, and in that passion there's a sense of rigidity and immobility because they want to study exactly what something is and what they think something is supposed to be . . . But I went through that. I mean it took me a while to kinda look in the mirror and say, f— it! I'm African American, you know . . . (Issa, New York, 2006)

Issa's rejection of 'traditionalists' came in the form of abandoning an 'obsession' with Africa and accepting what he calls his own 'African American reality'. Issa and Aisha argued that, physically, African Americans' dance evinces their unique bodily trajectories. Their bodies are different and evince their socio-cultural background in their dancing. So their 'traditional' moves will be different:

> When you see Africans dance, does it look the same as African Americans? No ... OK, so it has become something different that we haven't acknowledged or embraced. It's not the same. (Aisha, New York, 2006)

Acknowledging her difference, Aisha approaches the dances as a basis on which to innovate to express her 'African American reality':

> It's more about finding movements just to express what we've experienced as African Americans ... Not just as African people, because it's two different environments and many different experiences. (Aisha, New York, 2006)

Issa and Aisha's choice to embrace innovation was encouraged by the suggestions of West African dancers, the 'authorities' themselves. As West African 'traditional' dance companies were improvising, adjusting the dances for example to the context of the staged performance, they challenged ideas of 'authentic' and 'traditional' in West African dance. If 'traditionalists' aimed for a closer link to Africans, then it was perhaps more appropriate to follow the example of West African dance companies in innovation. Yet African American dancers have only recently taken this up:

> Before, you'd go to do a solo in class and the teacher would stop you and say 'that's not a correct traditional movement!' ... I think it's only in recent years, since the ballet companies have come around and done more creative stuff that people have started opening up. (Marie, New York, 2006)

The tension between 'traditionalists' and 'innovators' can be explained through what Fabre and O'Meally refer to as 'sites of memory' in African American culture:

> certain sites of memory were sometimes constructed by one generation in one way and then reinterpreted by another. These sites may fall unexpectedly out of grace, or be revisited suddenly and brought back to life. We found that *lieux de memoire* are constantly evolving new configurations of meaning, and that their constant revision makes them part of the dynamism of the historical process. (Fabre and O'Meally 1994: 9)

Seen this way, West African dances are 'sites of memory' that allow different generations to reinterpret what they are and should be about. I would argue further that it is not only generations that can affect and change the meaning of these dances; the New York example shows that, grounded in larger ideological trends, individual actors also do. Essentially the category 'innovators' glosses over the very different approaches of many teachers and students, while also ironing out differences amongst 'traditionalists'.

Concluding Uptown

To conclude, 'community' classes share certain common characteristics in the way they are set up and funded. They are hosted in public buildings in Harlem and taught primarily by African American teachers. The community feeling of the classes provides a joyful, relaxed and familiar atmosphere. The notion of community is asserted and reactivated through 'community announcements', the use of inclusive and thus exclusive kinship terminology and the evocation of common memories, knowledge and past experiences. Community classes also nurture a link to a monolithic Africa, as elements from different ethnicities are combined in the teaching of the dances. However in other Uptown classes, the teachers' agendas may de-emphasize the notions of community in order to promote other political and ideological agendas. These approaches may be considered 'innovative' by those who see the dances as a spatial and temporal link to Africa and argue for their 'traditional' practice. The tension between the 'there' and 'then' of 'traditionalists' and the 'here' and 'now' of 'innovators' replicates what Clifford calls the inherent, lived tension of Diaspora cultures that 'mediate, in a lived tension, the experiences of separation and entanglement, of living here and remembering/desiring another place' (Clifford 1997: 255). This tension 'is constituted negatively by experiences of discrimination and exclusion . . . [and] produced positively through identification with world-historical cultural/political forces, such as "Africa" or "China"' (ibid.: 256).

Downtown Students

So far I have explored how the sense of 'community' and a link to Africa is constituted positively within the exclusive dance-space of the community, and discussed how community is negotiated on the Downtown dance floor where it is one of the many understandings involved. In this section I will explore the other understandings of the Downtown dance floor. In contrast to Uptown community classes, Downtown classes attract a more diverse student body, thus becoming the grounds for different understandings to meet. While for Uptown participants West African dances are closely linked to community, non-African American students engage with the dances for what they describe as personal, physical and experiential reasons. Acknowledging the problems entailed in translating experiential concepts into anthropological discourse (Rada and Cruces 1994), I will attempt to provide some insight into their reasons for dancing.

Energy

> It's the energy of it . . . I had this one experience where the energy was so intense that . . . I wasn't completely thinking . . . like the movements were coming through me in this way that I had no control over it. I was moving and flaying my body around in this crazy way that was totally dictated by the music and . . . it was almost like a trance! (Amber, Dakar, 2006)

'Energy' is a concept that participants use to describe a personal or a communal experience of a certain dance-event. Energy is described as a force that is created in and affected by different parameters of a dance-event, such as the studio, the day and time of the class, the teacher, the drummers, the dancers or larger events (e.g. 11 September 2001). Some of these, like the drumming, the teacher and the combination of students, are seen as having more power over other elements. Energy is understood as dynamic, created in the intersubjective space of participants, with the ability to be 'inflated' or 'deflated'. Energy affects dancers who can in turn 'create' more energy. More important than how energy feels, is what it impels people to do. Energy can draw one more into one's dancing and thus make the experience of the class more enjoyable:

> one of the main reasons that I enjoy it so much is because of the energy . . . you know when I go to classes that don't have live music or where there are only a few students, it's a completely different experience. I really like it when there's a lot of people, a lot of energy, a lot of drummers. (Mary, Dakar, 2007)

The opposite scenario also exists, and the energy of the class may affect participants negatively. Thus energy is often used to describe a certain teacher or class positively, as in 'Vicky's got great energy' to advertise a class; but 'he brings the energy down', 'the energy is not right' or 'bad energy' can describe a class or teacher negatively. Personal experience can also be disassociated from the general energy of the class. Most often the term 'energy' is assigned to the drumming:

> Something about when all those instruments are played, is just like the energy of being lifted up . . . It's so much about the music, about the music and the dancing and the . . . Fhiouh! All your energy, you know! It's this amazing connection that happens between the dancer and the musicians. (Kathleen, Dakar, 2007)

The 'energy' of the drums was described by a dancer like 'an itch'. When she hears the drums she cannot stand still but has to get up and dance: 'the drum penetrates the body and that's something people who've never danced before cannot understand'. The drumming brings the dancer close to the percussionist, she explained: 'you get so close to each other, I mean it's really a way of connecting that I don't find I establish in any other way, this energy flow that happens, and when the music is good, I just, I just gotta dance!' For others, it is not the drumming itself but who the drummers are that creates the energy: 'You know you can feel certain energy from people in the room, and with this group of drummers in particular I feel so safe and such a positive energy and so not judged' (Claire, New York, 2008). The energy from the drumming is what, students often claim, distinguishes Sabar and Djembé from other physical activity. Thus different aspects of a dance-event can create more energy, which in turn affects these elements further. The drumming draws one to dance and as the dancing evinces students' appreciation of the drumming, the drummers will be drawn further into their drumming, which will in turn draw dancers further into their dancing and so on.[15] 'Energy' is also seen to be susceptible to personal moods, and so may predispose a dancer's experience of a certain class which however will not restrict her from understanding what the general energy of the class is, even if it is different from her own.

The Way It Makes Me Feel

Dancers also described their involvement in less 'exotic' terms, relating West African dances to the physical fulfilment they get from sports.[16] As one dancer explained, the 'workout' helps her to 'maintain her sanity':

> It's funny because my partners in the past, when I'm in a bad mood, they're always like 'Isn't there a dance class you can take? You haven't danced in three days; maybe you need to find a dance class.' I joke with people 'Oh! I'm a dance addict!', but if I don't dance for a while my body really craves it and misses it. (Mary, Dakar, 2007)

> If I don't do this for a while I feel a little bit 'out of whack', I'm missing something . . . Why this specifically? It's a very physical dance, the drums are live, you can feel them and it felt right in my body although I don't know if it was a different dance that I wouldn't enjoy that. (Nina, New York, 2006)

Dancers rationalized the feeling of happiness after class as the result of endorphins, the hormones produced during strenuous physical activity. However, not many dancers could explain why they chose West African dances over sports, except for the drumming:

Well, I feel like I'm addicted at this point. It is almost a form of religion for me. It elevates your spirit in a way that a lot of other things don't . . . I'm not a big runner . . . but the connection with the drums and the movements and just . . . all of it, it elevates your spirit in a way that you don't just get from a 'runners' high', you know, it's like a different, it's a deeper kind of thing. And yet there's still that endorphin rush of . . . Uh! (Mary, Dakar, 2007)

Like, if I had something weighing me down for a while, I had a lot of anxiety for a while, I'd come to dance class and I didn't have an ounce of anxiety . . . I just felt so free; and so when I would finish class I would leave literally high! Like you can't take a drug that can make you feel like that! (Claire, New York, July 2008)

Other participants described the classes as a way to escape their everydayness, to 'get out of one's head' and stop thinking:

I tend to over-think a lot of stuff and so dance gives me an outlet for just . . . I don't think at all when I'm dancing! It's just this detachment from your brain! It's like when you are a person who thinks a lot and you're like really analysing, you question everything . . . And I think that when you get into your body instead, you're like operating from here down and your head is just, I mean it's there! It's just not controlling every-thing. Yeah, it's not about logic – at all! No, no, no! That's the point! The point is to get out of that analytical, logical way of thinking and just be in your body. (Kathleen, Dakar, 2007)

Of course not everyone shares this view, as for beginners the class requires con-siderable concentration to remember steps and their sequence. For them, 'not thinking' is a luxury that only advanced students can afford.

Another attraction to West African dances seems to be its difference to ballet, to which comparisons were often drawn. Any adult could join West African dance classes, even with no previous training as a dancer: 'I was not a dancer growing up. In fact I took ballet when I was five or six and they kicked me out because I was always doing opposite things from what everyone else was doing' (Mary, Dakar, 2007). West African dances are seen as more approachable for beginners than ballet and modern as they do not demand previous experience or a life-long engagement. This does not mean that West African dance technique is easier than ballet but is rather a reflection of how the dances are institutionalized and taught in the U.S. Thus, in contrast to other dances, Sabar and Djembé are inclusive. Some dancers were attracted to West African technique because it is 'natural' and not 'counterintuitive' – both negative references to ballet:[17]

I really took to it, I really loved it. I found it very energizing and just the movement seemed simple and natural, not like counterintuitive . . . It just felt right in my body. It felt sort of therapeutic for me to dance, and the rhythm felt natural . . . it just felt good. (Laura, New York, 2006)

The notion of movement being 'natural' is very common in the discourses of participants and it is used by teachers in various pedagogical techniques, as we shall see later on.

Finally, while many of the reasons above also apply to Djembé, some students saw Sabar as an evolution from other West African dance forms. Sabar is considered to be complicated and difficult, requiring a more serious commitment. The drumming for example is not as 'straightforward' as in Djembé, and while movements tend to be repeated in Djembé they are always different in Sabar. In fact, the commitment required from students is what some teachers believe leads to a lesser demand for Sabar classes in New York. Yet for other students, Sabar is attractive precisely because it is challenging. Claire for example described her involvement as follows:

I feel physically fulfilled, intellectually fulfilled, emotionally, spiritually and even socially fulfilled through Sabar. Sabar meets all those different areas. I'm mentally stimulated. I'm challenged. In turn I feel good about myself. (Claire, New York, 2008)

Not everyone appreciates the challenge. Claire felt that even advanced dancers do not always appreciate teachers constantly showing new movements.

So far the socio-cultural background of the dance forms does not feature in the discourses of the participants as an important reason for their involvement. Instead reasons revolve around the uniqueness of the dance forms to combine a physical activity with drumming and the energy created in class. This does not necessarily mean that the dances' background does not matter. In fact some of the older participants cited the 'authenticity' and 'primitiveness' of the dances as reasons for their involvement, as will be discussed in the next chapter. It can further be argued that the attraction to the dance forms in New York is a way to experience cultural difference from the safe standpoint of one's own 'home'. However, it remains that in the students' voices, the background of the dances was not a prominent reason for learning Sabar, at least at first. This is not the case for the African American participants, however, for whom as already discussed the background of the dances, and their contemporary place, are very important. Hazzard-Gordon notes a similar discrepancy between African American and white participants' views in relation to social vernacular dances in the 1960s:

For the Afro-American dancer, social dancing is a central and fundamental carrier of meaning. The dance is more than personal entertainment, fun and good exercise. The dance is imbued with individual,
sociopsychological, cultural and political meaning. What the white
dancer perceives as the total reality, the movement itself is merely a contingent component of a wider reality. To the untrained white observer,
African movement appears independent of interlocking relationships
that permeate its presence. (Hazzard-Gordon 1985: 441)

The first part of this chapter explored the ways in which different understandings are negotiated on the dance floor in bodily terms, as groups or individuals
attempt to define the dance-events. As discussed, individual dancers may create a
hierarchy on the grounds of dance technique to position themselves in relation to
others, while at a group level some Uptown participants may 'mute' others in an
attempt to define the classes as 'community affairs'. In the following section I will
focus on the dancers who resist these two hierarchies, and explore the grounds
on which they do so.

Negotiating 'Community'

Lauren joined Sabar after years of ballet and modern dance, and by the time
I met her she was one of the best dancers of the New York scene. Lauren was
initially intimidated by the feeling of ownership and exclusion she felt from some
of the participants as a white student. Instead of challenging this, Lauren felt she
needed to justify her presence and right to participate:

You prove yourself through consistency or through ability or through
. . . I don't know . . . but I've earned my place and I've realized that a lot
of these people, like, I don't need their approval and I don't want, now
at this point, I don't want it. (Lauren, New York, 2008)

As an 'established' participant, Lauren felt she no longer needed to prove herself. She recognized however that her initial feelings of exclusion would be
replicated in the experiences of newcomers. Lauren's response resonates with
Herzfeld's analysis of women in Crete: 'While women have the means of expressing their resentment of male control and pretensions, they must always do
so by ostensibly endorsing what ideologically they subvert' (Herzfeld 1991:
94). Similarly, Lauren accepted the feeling of exclusion and responded to it
by proving her 'right' to participate. As Ardener argues, if muted groups 'wish
to communicate, [they] must express themselves in terms of this [dominant]
mode, rather than in ones which they might otherwise have generated independently' (S. Ardener 1993: 7), otherwise they will not be heard, or may be
misunderstood.

Lauren's confidence was also grounded on the close relationships she built with the 'authorities' in the class – the drummers, teachers and other advanced students that she evokes as 'support':

> Once I got through the intimidation and stuck with it, through the encouragement of the teachers and the drummers, you know, I realized I don't need their approval and I have every right to be here. And for me, I've really improved, I've worked really, really hard and yeah, like I deserve, you know, I have every right to be here as much as you do. (Lauren, New York, 2008)

Downtown teachers and drummers are often approached as mediators. They are also the only ones to explicitly address, encourage or discourage the silent negotiations of space and time. Thus teachers can affect to what extent a class will have an 'Afrocentric', according to some, or a 'community', according to others, feeling as they encourage or discourage students' attempts. Anna for example avoids a specific class because of its strong Afrocentric character and because the teacher does not challenge this. In contrast, Assane's class is preferred for being a 'relaxed', inclusive environment. The class combines elements from both settings as it is Uptown but is not free and draws a mixed group of students. There is rarely an attempt to define the class as a 'community' event, nor does it breed competition based on dancing abilities. In a student's words:

> I mean, I don't know because he's the only person who's got anything going on like that . . . It might just be that he's been able to capture the right combination . . . you've got a Harlem feel to his class but maybe because of the type of people he's been able to draw he doesn't get the people that are die hard Harlemites . . . 'I can't dance with them [non-community]; he doesn't get people with that mentality, he doesn't get the diehard 'Downtown divas' who at all costs must dance you out, he gets people that are right in the middle!

While teachers have the ability to mediate different groups and definitions of the purpose of the class, there can also be friction amongst them.

West African artists do not always share African Americans' concern with 'community'. In fact, André, like other Senegalese teachers, argues that Sabar is for everyone and should be shared indiscriminately. This is comforting to some students as it promotes a more inclusive class environment. André's choice not to make the dance form exclusive is also apparent in his choice not to teach Uptown:

> What is stopping them from coming Downtown? They only want it for themselves. When you're sharing it's not about black or white, its for everybody, you know? (André, New York, 2008)

André's resistance, however, reveals another point of tension, this time between West Africans and African Americans.[18] West African teachers cannot afford to exclude African American students as they know 'that Africa sells very well . . . in North America' (Stoller 2002: 73). This forces West African migrants into an ironic situation where they:

> find themselves both catering to and resisting a stereotypical image of themselves . . . that both benefits them economically and denies their cultural specificity . . . Knowing something about the history and plight of African Americans a few . . . migrants accept the fact that the 'Africa' African Americans 'need' is not the one they know. In the Harlem market context they are prepared to renounce recognition of the complexities of the Africa from which they come, and make a gift of the more unencumbered significance it has acquired in the local community. (Coombe and Stoller 1994, in Stoller 2002: 82)

Thus to an extent West Africans cater to the African American approach, mediating between students' unique views of Sabar while also avoiding discouraging anyone from attending. For Lauren, André also actively discourages the 'divas': 'André just . . . like rolled his eyes in the "you gotta be kidding me, like get over yourself"'. André's reaction here, performed or not, maintains a balance. He does not openly confront the 'divas' but distances himself from them, thus 'neutralizing' the purpose of the class for those not sharing the competitive aspect of these dancers. There is a strong economic incentive for André to make his classes inclusive and thus available to a broader market. This is to a certain extent linked to André's cultural capital as a *géwël*, as the traditional relationship between *géwël* and *geér* demands financial compensation for services rendered from a *géwël* to one's patron and audience.

In addition to authorities like teachers and drummers, students may also resist attempts to define an event as a 'community' affair. An example of this was through an email exchange following a four-day festival in Boston that was circulated to New York's African dance community. The festival included dancing and drumming classes of Sabar, Djembé and Kutiro, with dancers and drummers from Guinea and Senegal.[19] Festivals like these bring together students from different states and are also an occasion for friends to meet. Following the four days of dancing and drumming, a 'thank you' email, addressed to the organizers, was sent to an email list, an excerpt from which read:

> There is nothing like dancing with family in different places, and it was great to see family from all over the states joining together for a great time . . . such a special moment uniting Africans and African Americans. All in all, I had a great time dancing, singing and drumming with my brothers and sisters, and I can't wait for next year's event!

The female participant, presumably African American, here proclaimed the event's purpose to 'unite Africans and African Americans' and employed kinship terminology to exclude those who did not fit the 'family' category. The email received a reply by the African American wife of the Senegalese organizer who resisted the attempt to define the event as a community affair by giving a different picture of the event, the demographics of the participants, and by glossing the event as cosmopolitan:

> We would like to send our most sincere thanks to all of the people who came to the second annual Festival! It was truly a success with participants who came from across the U.S. and from Italy, Greece, Togo and Montreal!

The organizer's attempt to highlight international participants can be merely seen as an attempt to not discourage future patrons. But it also reflects the reality of the demographics of that conference. Participants came from a variety of backgrounds. The organizer's reply, beyond presenting a more realistic account of the attendance of the conference, also redefined the purpose of the class. Her reply silenced the previously defining voice that portrayed the event as a 'community' affair and redefined it as cosmopolitan.

An Invested Approach

Having discussed how space and time are negotiated to position participants on the grounds of dancing abilities or to define the classes as 'community' affairs, I discussed how they also resist these two hierarchies. Here I turn to a third hierarchy, invoked by those who promote a more 'serious' approach to their practice. In addition to attending Sabar classes regularly, Claire tried to learn as much as possible outside the class. This included staying 'in touch' with the latest choreographies as they became popular in Senegal:

> You know Kelly and I will watch these videos that the guys will bring back from Senegal and we're like 'Alright, how do we do this?' And we'll stand in the living room trying to figure out how to do it . . . literally we'll go back over and we'll teach ourselves because I don't know . . . I want to learn more, I wanna have a vocabulary, I want it to keep growing.

As part of her learning, Claire built close friendships with drummers, teachers and their families, started learning Wolof and travelled to Senegal as a guest of a New York teacher's family. Similar to Claire, Michelle's approach to Sabar contains an implicit critique of other, less invested approaches to West African dances (e.g. Jenkins 1995). Michelle is an African American, and criticizes Afrocentrism and the 'mixing' of elements from different traditions as a 'lazy' claim to origins:

You know sometimes, especially with the language problem, I find being African American and able to speak one African language I'm a little biased because I look at other African Americans and I see a lot of . . . we're quick to go to South Africa or Nigeria or Ghana 'cos there's no language barrier; so when dealing with francophone countries it's a little different because there's a lot of things we don't pick up!

Michelle criticizes those who attempt to build a bridge to 'Africa' without investing the effort. She believes that this lack of interest for a 'proper' approach to learning also defines the way West African dances are taught, where aspects from different ethnic traditions are mixed and used in different contexts. An example of this is the standardized use of the Liberian term *'lapa'* throughout West African dance classes – including Sabar – to denote one's wrap skirt (in Senegal a wrap is most commonly referred to as *'pagne'*). Michelle's criticism and approach to the dance forms can be seen as an attempt to build a more substantial bridge to Africa, which at the same time sets her apart from other less invested approaches. By acknowledging and aligning herself with other dancers who take a similar approach she establishes a new hierarchy on the grounds of an invested approach to learning the dance forms.

Conclusion

In this chapter I have explored the way New York classes are organized, taught and understood by the different participants involved. To a certain extent, the geographical, socio-economic and intellectual setting of the classes predefines the meaning of the classes for the participants. Thus the different voices about dance are linked to political relations specific to each context. However, the political geography of the class is also linked to the larger socio-cultural geography of New York City and to broader historical and political discourses. Sabar classes force dancers into homogeneity. Participants negotiate time and space on the dance floor to re-choreograph larger socio-political relationships and to assert themselves in the class, individually and/or as a group. Thus time and space can be negotiated to denote one's dancing abilities and establish oneself as a good dancer or to 'mute' others and express claims of ownership. Some of the ways in which the 'community' perspective is expressed in class invert conventional hierarchies. African American participants, a 'mute' group in U.S. history and society, 'silence' 'Others' and define the class as a 'community' affair by manipulating space and time. Certain community members also actively distance themselves and/or silence attempts to define the classes as community affairs. In a more powerful position to offer a definition of the forms are the West African artists who Other participants often approach as authorities. West African teachers and drummers do not necessarily share a community agenda but at the same time cannot afford to isolate them. New York City classes thus become the grounds for the negotiation of present-day socio-cultural relations and the attempt to re-choreograph history and politics within the geography of the dance floor. Finally, dancers may ignore and often contest the aforementioned hierarchical structures by evoking new ones, as for example by positioning themselves as invested students of Sabar.

Notes

1. Wax cotton fabrics with colourful prints found throughout West and East Africa, used to make matching outfits.

2. Stevie Wonder wrote 'Happy Birthday' in 1981 to promote his campaign to establish a national holiday celebration for the birthday of Dr Martin Luther King Jr. The holiday was implemented by President Reagan and was first held on 20 January 1986. This song was used in all Downtown and Uptown West African dance classes for birthday celebrations, highlighting the link of West African dance classes to African American history and memory.

3. Orbe and Harris define interracial communication as 'the transactional process of message exchange between individuals in a situational context where racial difference is perceived as a salient factor by at least one person' (2008: 6).

4. I explore the Uptown context through the Djembé classes as, with the exception of a paid class at the YMCA, Sabar was not taught Uptown at the time of this fieldwork. I was told that Sabar was taught Uptown in the past but that the migration of West African dancers in the 1990s settled its teaching Downtown. At the time of this fieldwork an African American dancer was trying to establish a free, weekly Sabar class Uptown but was not able to gather enough students.

5. Thus the term 'community' is used here as an emic category in the way it is used by the participants, and not as an analytical term (for the latter, see Cohen 1985).

6. See also Dixon-Gottschild (2003: 3); on ballet bodies, see Wulff (1998).

7. Kwanzaa is an African American, 'secular' holiday which starts on 26 December and lasts for a week. It was invented in 1966 by Ron Karenga, a leader of a black nationalist group called 'US' (United Slaves), who in 2008 became the head of the Black Studies department at California State University, Long Beach. The celebration combines elements from different African traditions. Kwanzaa is often criticized on the grounds that 'its instant myth-making fabricates a false history' (Economist 1994). Regardless, it is estimated that eighteen million people celebrate it and so it is also a financially lucrative event (ibid.).

8. Wilkinson, however, argues that among African Americans, Afrocentricity in one's way of dressing for example no longer denotes nostalgia but has instead moved mainstream and become an 'exciting new trend' (Wilkinson 1996). In contrast, for Jenkins, heritage and 'authenticity' should not be compromised by a drive for consumption but instead approached critically (Jenkins 1995).

9. The notion of 'community feeling' is also used in popular imagination in reference to music from Africa. It is criticized by Ebron (2002: 48) who argues that such a reading restricts alternative understandings of music from Africa.

10. She uses the example of Malcolm X who having, in his words, 'acquired all the other fashionable ghetto adornments – the zoot suits and conk . . . liqueur, cigarettes, then

reefers – all that to erase my embarrassing background . . . I still harboured one secret humiliation: I could not dance' (Haley 1966: 56). Hazzard-Gordon argues that Malcolm X was still an outsider because of his inability to dance, which was a result of his integration into American culture. His inability to dance evinced that one's cultural base is not black, that one has taken on another cultural identity (Hazzard-Gordon 1985: 431).

11. Gilroy's *Black Atlantic* aimed to move 'the more familiar uni-directional notion of diaspora as a form of dispersal which enjoys an identifiable and reversible originary moment, into a much more complex "chaotic" model in which unstable "strange attractors" are also visible' (Gilroy 1993: 22).

12. The need to 'defend' dances from Africa in terms of technical difficulty and to carve out respect for them in American popular culture is a recurring theme in the discourse of participants. One teacher argued that the fact that West African dances are now taught in dance studios Downtown has helped positively in the recognition of the technical difficulty of the dances. Another occasion of bringing popular recognition to West African dances was on 15 July 2009, when Djembé featured on the American reality show 'So You Think You Can Dance'. One of the show's critics emphasized that 'African dance' technique is the basis of many popular American dance forms like hip hop and jazz, and thus deserves more attention. After the show, emails circulated amongst the African dance community of New York City congratulating the choreographer Jeffrey Page for bringing African dance to the attention of Americans. Jeffrey Page had previously incorporated Djembé moves in pop star Beyoncé's choreography, in the video *Déjà Vu*.

13. Lamban is a Malinke dance which, according to most teachers, comes from Mali.

14. The attempt to engage and re-appropriate all things African, including the conversion to Islam and relocation to Africa, was exemplified by Malcolm X.

15. It is worth emphasizing that this view of the students may not be shared by the drummers.

16. This view challenges conventional anthropological approaches that treat sport and dance as distinct, a point previously made by Dyck and Archetti (2003).

17. Ballet is discussed as 'unnatural' also amongst ballerinas (Wulff 1998: 105).

18. The relationship between African Americans and West Africans has been discussed extensively in the literature, and Perry (1997), Foner (2001) and Waters (1999) have noted the discomfort expressed by West Africans and West Indians for being grouped by North Americans as African Americans for their skin colour. For the Senegalese this discomfort may arise from the fact that they act according to Islamic ideas and concepts of reciprocity and hard work (Perry 1997), notions they do not feel they share with African Americans (Malcomson 1996: 44, Perry 1997: 15; see also Abdullah 2009). Waters notes West Indian migrants' attempts to distance themselves from African Americans (Waters 1999: 74), arguing that African Americans are much more prone to see racial solidarity over ethnic differences than West Indians, who tend to disassociate themselves explicitly from African Americans. This is similar to the Senegalese and other West African teachers in New York who also at times disassociate themselves from the community aspect of West African dance classes embraced by African Americans.

19. Kutiro is a dance-rhythm form mostly found in the Casamance region of Southern Senegal.

Chapter 3

Navigating Transatlantic Flows

Imagine . . . waking up to the roosters crowing in the yard . . . imagine spending your days receiving personalized dance and drum instruction from master artists . . . sitting on the sun-splashed shores . . . the excitement of the drums beating. Imagine the sights and smells of the market place where you bargain over brightly coloured cloth . . . dancing to the drums under the light of the moon . . . imagine making new friends and developing new cultural understandings, your tongue twisting over new sounds . . . trying new foods, eating from a communal bowl. Imagine what a wonderful experience you will have when you come with us to Guinea! (Email to the yahoo emailing list AfricanDance_New York, April 2007)

I needed to understand the authenticity, the genuine-ness of the dance right inside the culture. (Karen, Dakar, 2007)

First time I went to West Africa was such an amazing experience! We stayed at the teacher's actual home in Conakry, with his family . . . fifteen of us, five from Japan, some Americans and one from England. Everyday we had one drum and two dance classes. We took trips out to the countryside, went to the beach or to buy fabric . . . It's a real eye opener to go to West Africa just to see what it's like. (John, New York, 2006)

Since his first trip to Guinea, John has also visited Senegal on his own or as a guest of family members of New York teachers. John is not a typical New York student of West African dance as he is one of the very few male ones. John is not untypical, however, in choosing to travel to West Africa. Students travel to West Africa on their own or in trips organized by New York teachers to learn Djembé and Sabar in 'context'.

The trips are advertised through websites, emails, brochures and classes, marketed by teachers, their partners and former participants.[1] The promotion of the trips is one part, and for some students the beginning, of a longer process that maintains an exchange of people and dance forms between the U.S. and the West African coast. Students travel, either as part of these organized trips, or independently, staying with contacts or family members of their New York teachers. They attend daily dance and drum lessons and visit local performances and ceremonies. A common stereotype amongst female students, and one they openly joke about, is that in West Africa they will fall in love with an 'African man'. This becomes reality for some women and at times the relationships are important enough that they choose to stay longer in West Africa or to bring their partners back to the United States. Marriage then becomes one way for West African artists to migrate. A second route has been 'artists' visas', where again U.S. students' help is very important. Once in the U.S., teachers receive help from friends, partners and older migrants on how to set up and manage classes and workshops. If the teacher becomes popular, develops a following of students and is legally able to leave and return to the U.S., he can choose to organize trips to West Africa. In doing so, new students will travel to West Africa, thus maintaining a movement of people and dance forms, giving this movement the form of a loop. This is not of course a comprehensive account of everyone involved with West African dances. Many students never travel to West Africa, while others cross paths with this loop or join in at different points. Moreover, I have not included African American students in this analysis. This is because of the place Africa occupies in African American memory and identity, which leads to unique incentives for travelling (see Bruner 1996, Johnson 1999, Ebron 2002, Essien 2008; and, for a literary account, Angelou 1987). Here I explore the social settings this loop passes through, the conditions that allow it to exist and the understandings involved in this movement. I argue that the discrepancy between individual views and kinds of knowledge at different levels of involvement with this loop point against a reading of the consuming West and a consumed Africa (Mudimbe 1988), which has been used to analyse representations of Africa and to explain North–South romantic relations. Instead, I illustrate that the relationships between those involved reveal multiple levels of interaction.

The Search for 'Context' and 'Authenticity'

> I'm really interested in learning the depth of the dances, what they mean and how they're expressed in context . . . and not just physically how to do them. (Laura, New York, 2006)[2]

Laura here is expressing a very common view amongst New York participants. West African dances are not simply a physical practice. They are attached to a body of knowledge and set of other related practices and conventions: the 'context'. For the proper practice of the dances one needs to also study their 'context'. What kind of 'context' do participants invoke and consider authentic? In social analysis when choosing what to consider as context we are already involved in interpretation (Dilley 1999a). We choose to make certain connections and accept disconnections between what we study and what surrounds it. Thus while context is evoked in order to determine meaning, context is itself part of the meaning produced. This makes 'context' a problematic notion even if it is rarely accepted as such (ibid.). Furthermore, choosing a certain 'context' over others also implicates power (Hobart 1986). Here I am interested in participants' contextualizing moves and consequently their acts of interpretation as well as the ways in which power and economics are involved in the process. An implicit theme in this discussion is the concept of 'authenticity' which, as discussed, I approach in a constructivist manner (Reisinger and Steiner 2006a), that is, as a category of the participants and not an analytical, objective quality of the forms (see Introduction).

Amongst U.S. participants only the older ones voiced 'authenticity' as a motive to travel to West Africa, perhaps reflecting earlier popular discourses surrounding the dance forms. In contrast, younger participants never made explicit claims to authenticity even though it seemed implicit in their search for 'context', in expecting and evaluating certain settings as more appropriate than others. Similar to 'authenticity', 'context' here features as an 'emic' term, a category of the students and not an analytical term.

Context-less New York

The desire for 'context' is nurtured in the way the dances are taught in New York. Teachers 'make it clear that in Guinea people don't just dance for fun but there is always meaning behind it' (Laura, New York, 2006). West African dances in New York are seen as 'context-less'. Their practice is incomplete or 'not the real thing'. One can learn the physical part of the dances, have fun with them and build friendships but something will be missing. In contrast, a more 'serious' approach includes the body of knowledge attached to the dances: 'The context is REALLY important. That gets lost if you're a person who's just taking a dance class like I would take an aerobics class. It's not an aerobics class!' (Mary, Dakar, 2006).[3]

However the 'context' of the dances varies, signifying at times the occasion of performance or the geographical and ethnic origins of a dance, through to historical and cultural explanations of specific steps (e.g. this movement is inspired by the planting season and imitates sowing). The 'context' is often linked to Africa as a traditional place and a rural, agricultural lifestyle, an image that is at times challenged by teachers giving contradicting information: 'For all the dancing I've done I'm embarrassingly bad at dance names. I'd like to attribute this to different teachers using different names [and] definitions of what a dance is' (Julia, Dakar, 2006).[4] The inconsistency at times frustrates students, highlighting their expectations that 'authentic' and 'traditional' ought to have a definite, consistent background.

These expectations do not allow for the 'messy' and complex ways through which the dances are related ethnically and politically. With state boundaries cutting across ethnicities, attributing a dance to a country can be problematic. Yet dances are often discussed as 'Malian' or 'Guinean' thus blurring the fact that they may belong to more than one country or that they come from a specific region or ethnicity. Thus West Africa's historical and ethnic complexity leads to contradicting stories of 'context'. Teachers' inability to provide consistent information may also result from the recent popularity of the dances. Specialist knowledge of the dances has traditionally been the cultural capital of the *griots*. The increasing international demand has brought more individuals from non-*griot* backgrounds to dance professionally. Yet proficiency in the dances does not guarantee knowledge of their background. Thus, while West African dances in New York are promoted as attached to a 'context', and while the students often demand context, context is not always consistent between teachers.

The 'context' is also used to differentiate students from each other. The background of the dances is not available in New York but rests in West Africa for the student to discover. As travelling to West Africa is a financial, timely and physical commitment (e.g. vaccinations) that not everyone can afford, the inaccessibility renders the acquisition of 'context' special and elevates those who have accessed it. This resembles Appadurai's (1986) discussion of luxury goods that differentiates those who can afford to consume them from those who cannot. Luxury goods are a 'specific "register" of consumption' (ibid.: 38) rather than special in themselves. It is their quality of being expensive, limited and related to personality or the body that allows them to be used to distinguish those who can afford them. Similarly, for the New York participants, acquiring the 'context' defines the committed students against the rest and is often evoked in New York dance classes through the occasional use of Wolof greetings and traditional wax clothes. Thus, invoking and appropriating elements of the 'context' of the dance form has direct implications on the self. The context can be used as currency, to legitimize self to oneself and to others in the practice of the dance forms.

The emphasis on 'context' seems to echo popular discourses on political correctness and anthropologists' attempts to undo misunderstandings. As Kaeppler argued, from 1950 onwards 'the Boasian and Herskovitsian emphasis on cultural relativism was widespread in America' and students of that tradition were permeated with the 'doctrine that dance and music must be considered in the context of the society of which they are parts' (Kaeppler 2000: 119). As many participants I interviewed came from a liberal arts university background, their understanding of the dance forms may reflect this. This approach for example underlines the way West African dance is taught at Hunter College (CUNY) where the classes include information on the dances' background. The course can be used to satisfy curriculum requirements, as can a language, literature, history or anthropology course – an option not available for other dance modules. Promoting West African dances as part of a larger body of knowledge contrasts them with a lay Euro-American understanding of dance where dance is limited to physical competence. This contrast essentially reaffirms West African dances as intrinsically different from other dance forms, as 'Other'. As intrinsically Other affairs, West African dances are to be approached in terms of 'context' and their practice in New York is thus limited to their physical aspect.

The Promised 'Context'

> I wanted people to see the real culture. They learn the dancing, the drumming, the culture, our hospitality, the food ... In Senegal they have paintings, masked arts, a lot of beautiful nature, beautiful islands, nice animals, beautiful villages... There's Gorée island,[5] good to see because the island is the original, like it was many years ago. (New York Sabar teacher, New York, 2006)

Teachers, brochures and websites promise a 'context' for the dances in West Africa[6] which, includes the African landscape, the 'reality' of African life and the more immediate practice of the forms. In the discourses of these advertisements, the African landscape encourages an organic experience and proximity to nature. The traveller is absorbed in a rich sensual interaction with nature, from the morning when 'roosters are crowing', through to 'smells of the market place', sun-splashed shores, drums beating, and opportunities for 'sitting under a waterfall' and 'dancing under the moon'.[7] The workshops are either located in, or include the experience of, the rural setting: 'Our land is about a mile from a remote, traditional Fulani village'.[8] Life in Africa begins with the family: 'Guests stay with Allasane's family at our compound' where they physically absorb culture through the host's home-cooked foods: 'Delicious Senegalese food is prepared daily by Ousmane's sisters'. The hosts give special entry to the culture – 'our visitors are not tourists' but 'guests [who] return from this trip with lifetime friends'. The trips offer a privileged perspective and a deep interaction, 'a total immersion experience into African culture' providing the guest with 'a realistic picture of African life'.

Yet, none of this is imposed on the guests. These advertisements are aware of who they cater to and where the potential 'guests' come from, and make a point not to discomfort the guest: 'accommodations are simple but comfortable'. They remind the traveller to bring, along with the malaria prophylaxis, 'an open mind and a flexible attitude' as 'please remember you are visiting another culture'. This advertises that Africa is available for controlled consumption at levels that are comfortable for the consuming guest, who remains in control of the interaction: 'receiving personalized dance instruction, ordering a custom-made drum. There's lots of leisure time to walk on the beach'. The trip is thus not only about Africa and the dances, but also about the individual willing to experience them: 'Experience [at] first hand the hospitality . . . Stay a week, stay a month. We welcome you to paradise!'[9] Accounts from past travellers are often included in the advertisements and, as expected, they remain close to the above themes. The landscape is given spiritual qualities, and so is filled with 'well-being and energy'. The people appear exceptionally 'humane' and value 'human beings above all else, their warmth, generosity, calmness and ability to really listen' standing in direct contrast to the individualistic Western urban environment.[10] The promised Africa appears as the extreme Other to New York students' lives and is targeting that audience. This way it perpetuates the dichotomy that, Mudimbe argues, emerged with the colonizing structure and has resulted in a system of 'a great number of current paradigmatic oppositions . . . traditional versus modern; oral versus written and printed; agrarian and customary communities versus urban and industrialized civilization' (Mudimbe 1988: 4). Similar to other cultural tours, the Africa offered is very much the one expected in the imaginations of its visitors, as created through the media, anthropologists and tourist guides (Ebron 2002, Urry 1990).

A prominent theme in these advertisements is that dance and drumming are everywhere in Africa: 'you are constantly surrounded by it; very small children and old people always seem to be dancing'. Traditional authority settings of dance are used by local artists as cultural capital which they advertise to international students:

> The . . . family are *griots* . . . *griots* are recognized throughout Africa as keepers of the history of their people, through music and the oral traditions. Historically musicians and *griots* are transmitters of wisdom . . . For ten years now Abdoulaye has brought his students to Conakry not only to teach them the art of traditional Djembé drumming but to do so within the same culturally rich community and environment he also learned from.

The students are promised the traditional learning setting of the artists themselves, the *griot* family environment.

However, this 'context' is ignored if there are other qualities on offer, as for example when an artist is reputed for his artistic competence and teaching skills:

> Hailing from the golden era of the Senegalese Ballet . . . Thousands of students worldwide have experienced the unmatched expertise and traditional knowledge of . . . A fortunate generation of us have trained with this dynamic duo . . . providing training and performance of the many traditions of Song, Dance and Drum by the Mali empire still yielding some of the community's best-trained dancers![11]

Interestingly, advertisements that emphasize dance skills are targeting advanced students, as for them learning with Master dancers is an important reason to travel to West Africa. Thus, the aforementioned 'context' is used instrumentally and is targeting novices. The 'context' is an established selling point that attracts students to West Africa, thus providing an income for the hosting families. Instead the teachers not involved in these trips highlighted the instrumentality of the context, arguing that what is promised cannot be delivered in such a short time. In contrast, they considered as valuable the opportunity to learn from different teachers on these trips, a point shared by advanced students but which is not, however, advertised. The above problematizes the importance of 'context', bringing the aforementioned tension between 'context' and 'competence' to the foreground.

Students' Many Contexts

The advertised Africa is the familiar Africa represented in popular culture, media, novels, films and travel writings, and has been the subject of much scholarship. The artefacts and themes of these representations have been approached as a way to understand the discursive practices that brought them into existence, as for example the colonial and postcolonial agenda (Mudimbe 1988), contemporary popular American culture (Mayer 2002) or the in-between space of the 'popular imagination' and 'scientific knowledge' in a specific period of time (Coombes 1994). More relevant for this analysis are the works of Ebron (2002) and Castaldi (2006) that explore how these themes are represented in performances to international audiences. Castaldi analyses Senghor's writings, as she argues that they have influenced the character of the performance, and explores the critiques that feature on the programme notes on the basis that they determine the audiences' understanding (Castaldi 2006). Ebron on the other hand looks at a variety of 'performances' exploring themes produced in the anthropological literature on music and themes created in the performances of Mande musicians from The Gambia for Western audiences. In contrast to Castaldi, Ebron does not assume a homogenous understanding of the audience and instead recognizes an 'enactment of various "Africas"' (Ebron 2002: 63). Here I contribute to this literature by moving the research focus from the analysis of discourses and observation of performances to engaging with the consumers of these 'Africas' and by exploring their understandings. In the process I illuminate participants' individual perspectives, which remains a neglected area in the literature on African representations.

The 'context' takes different forms in the voices of participants. The context anticipated by those travelling to West Africa for the first time is very close to the themes promoted in the brochures. The dances are thought to originate from a traditional, rural setting and are performed in ceremonies, rituals and occasions linked to agriculture. In Mary's words, 'Haki Lambe is done at harvest time. They do it as an offering to the harvest, as a blessing' (Mary, Dakar, 2007). For those students, 'context' denotes aspects not immediately observable and they speak of the dances as being 'symbolic', having 'depth' and 'communicating a particular story'. Students considered important 'the stories behind them [dances]', emphasizing a historical understanding of the dances and the 'authentic context', the original reasons for their performance. Yet, when interrogating this symbolic significance, the responses collapsed historical significance and symbolism with the present occasion of performance – for example, 'the harvest' – thus suggesting that what is observable now has always been the case. This understanding of a static history that collapses past and present, and fixes time to the land of West Africa, makes the 'context' conveniently available to the observing visitor who can acquire it by travelling to West Africa.

However, for those with a longer experience in West Africa, the 'context' included contemporary life, politics and economy: 'Conakry is a harsh and ugly place. Dancing is like a flower there' (Maya, New York, 2006). Dance-events are organized to support political leaders or for 'white people who come to study dancing and music'. In these cases, the 'context' refers to contemporary performance settings and is de-romanticized. Context here is what can be observed by being physically present at a dance-event and so experience is considered very important 'It takes years! It's not something that you just, like, know or even read about in a book!' (Mary, Dakar, 2007). One may be told what the dances are about but that knowledge remains 'abstract'. Instead, one can learn through experience, not only of performances but of everyday life. For one participant this was grounded on the view that everyday activities are linked to dance movements in the way they make use of the body. In this case, one accumulates 'context' through extended stay and experience of the dance forms.[12] Experiencing Senegalese life means living the way local people do and engaging in their everyday activities. As Mary describes: 'we stayed with a family and so really got the real deal – the toilets, the mosque, the imams waking you up in the morning'. Similarly, French dancer Ann-Sophie explained how her learning Sabar was intrinsically linked to learning how Senegalese people live:

I lived in a Senegalese family, 100 per cent like them. I ate *ceebujen*, washed myself with a bucket [laughs] . . . learned Wolof.[13] For me when you approach a dance, you approach a culture. When you see a woman doing Sabar, she is wearing all her culture and way of being in her everydayness. That, only from lived experience, day by day you can feel it and integrate a part of that culture.[14]

For Ann-Sophie, engagement with everyday practices allows a gradual appropriation of movements that are linked to the dances. What is interesting in this approach is that it is the living habits of the poor that are thought to allow such insight. In contrast, I never heard participants claim they could achieve the same by living in a middle- or upper-class Senegalese household.

At first sight, this seems to relate to the traditional conceptions of the 'caste' of the *griots* – to which dancers and drummers belong – who are traditionally associated with a lower status. However, the fact that *griots* have often enjoyed financial wealth renders the above perspective problematic. In addition, dancing is not exclusive to *griots*, as many Senegalese from other backgrounds dance Sabar and Mbalax recreationally. The idea that one can only learn Sabar through the habits of the poor does not reflect the socio-economic standing of *griots* but relates to popular conceptions of the 'real' Africa where the daily habits of a traditional and simple lifestyle are considered really African and not those of the 'contaminated' Westernized, middle- and upper-class Africans. Mudimbe makes a similar point in how Africans are represented in academia, where 'strangely enough, Africanists – and among them anthropologists – have decided to separate the "real" African from the Westernized African and to rely strictly upon the first' (Mudimbe 1988: x).[15] This 'real' African, the real Other, seems to persist and attract foreign students of dance. An intrinsic part of this 'real' Africa is dancing and drumming.

The idea that 'all Africans dance' resonates both with local discourses and popular representations of Africa. *Griots* are believed to have a natural predisposition to dancing and drumming, as they are 'in their blood' (Chapter 1). Others rationalize this claim, pointing out that not all *griots* dance and arguing instead that dancing is an acquired property. Historically, ideological and political movements have used drumming and dancing to celebrate African identity (Castaldi 2006, Neveu Kringelbach 2005). As a result, they emphasized biological distinctions between 'Us' (Africa) and 'Them' (the West), which are still prominent in the discourses of those involved with the arts. As a Senegalese drummer explained:

[When] the women grind the millet [makes rhythmic pounding sound] all the kids in the house feel this. When a woman is pregnant, when you are born, the babies on the backs of the mothers . . . Here, everything is rhythm. It's the system.

Similar ideas are replicated in the discourses of foreigners: 'The minute they can walk, they dance' (Mexican dancer, Dakar, 2007), and 'It's in their blood and genes! It's in every cell of their being you know!' (U.S. student, Dakar, 2007). It is difficult to determine to what extent these ideas reflect local understandings and traditional conceptions of 'caste' or pan-Africanist political agendas and popular representations of African dance by the West. However the idea that dance and drums are everywhere in 'Africa' serves to establish teachers' authority, promotes trips to West Africa and appears to be shared by many students who travel to West Africa.

Looking at what students choose to consider as the 'context' of West African dances problematizes the notion of 'context'. The brochures advertising trips to West Africa promise a 'context' of the familiar, romantic Africa, of the sensual landscape and of the people with a communal, rural lifestyle. This 'context' seems to target new students as the more advanced ones privilege the dancing over the 'context' and choose to embark on the trips for the reputation of the teachers. Once in West Africa, however, the 'context' takes many forms in the voices of the participants. Some students reiterate the same popular representations while others use 'context' to refer to the daily habits of Senegalese, including the popular view that Africa is saturated by rhythm and dance. Thus performing everyday living habits, albeit only of the poor, inscribes one with rhythm and an ability to dance. However, the 'context' changes in relation to a student's length of stay in West Africa, and so in the voices of those with a longer experience, the 'context' includes political events and the urban environment where international students, like themselves, are an important aspect of dance-events.

In participants' contextualizing moves there is a 'lay' appropriation of anthropological concepts. Perhaps this approach is invited by the fact that the dances are distinctly Other. The literature on tourism has compared tourists and anthropologists in their search for the 'authentic Other' in distant, exotic lands (Crick 1989, Harkin 1995, Frankland 2001). While I would hesitate to consider the participants of this network tourists, since the length of their stay often renders the place visited into a place of residence, they do share certain elements with anthropologists in the way they go about acquiring 'context' that is reminiscent of anthropology's methodology of participant observation.[16] The comparison between tourists, dance students and anthropologists also resonates in the way locals and participants conceptualize these three categories. Dance has been an established commodity for tourists. Finally, the dances gain further significance as participants interpret their engagement personally. The dances are viewed through students' personal trajectories and approaches to life, and so while their understandings are informed by various discourses on West African dances, the dances do not resist individual interpretations.

Karen, for example, was in her late 40s, from the U.S., and had first travelled to Guinea over a decade earlier with fellow students. She worked and lived there for five years before moving to Dakar. She spoke about Guinea with nostalgia. As she explained, she was not yet ready to move to the U.S. She felt an integral part of Guinea's dance scene and missed her friends: 'I just feel psychologically almost more Guinean now inside myself than American. Although I'm still very American, when I'm in Guinea I feel completely at home.' Karen described her engagement as a result of two driving forces in her life: karma and a commitment to authenticity. She had discovered West African dance in the U.S. with a teacher who was 'pretty good . . . for a white woman'. Karen's love for dance was the result of karma. As she put it, she had the 'seed that was in fertile soil', so when she discovered Djembé she acted upon her quest for authenticity and went to Guinea. Karen was attracted to the challenging nature of the dances, which cultivate a feeling of self-growth – 'it's almost the reason I live at this point' – and to the connection between the drummers and dancers: 'this energetic flow that happens . . . when the music is good I just gotta dance!'. Dance keeps her healthy and happy, and is a priority in her life: 'It is all about dancing and dancing with Africans at this point!' Other than a personal quest for authenticity, another aspect to Karen's involvement seemed to be the person she is when she is in West Africa. With a U.S. salary, Karen was rich in Guinea's economy, which enabled her to help her friends financially: 'Guinea is a very hard place to live, and I was in a position to be able to help a lot of people. That was really good and I'm still doing that.' This of course also allowed her certain privileges such as financing dance-events like *doudounbas* and paying for her teachers' trips for her lessons.[17] She saw herself as an important aspect of the local dance community: 'I'm an integral, I'm part of the weave now, I know I have family there – I'm just a part of the artists' scene'.

Feeding the Process

Relationships, like Karen's, between foreign students and locals are very important as they contribute to the transatlantic movement of people and dances. West African artists' relationships with foreigners often materialize into visas. The U.S. nationality of American women endows them with social and geographic mobility to enter and leave West African countries relatively free from trouble. This is reflected in their ability to reside in West Africa for however long they wish, and their ability to choose to stay on once already there.[18] In contrast, the West African artists' nationalities do not grant them similar freedoms. It is difficult for them to travel abroad on financial grounds, but more importantly, their nationality limits their power to cross the borders of certain countries. This brings to the forefront Hannerz's (1989) distinction between centre and periphery, a relationship that is still relevant today, affecting differently the mobility of cultural forms and, in this case, people.

Two common ways for West African artists to reach the U.S.A. have been to obtain an 'Artist Visa' or to enter as the fiancé or spouse of a U.S. citizen. U.S. immigration provides individual or group visas to artists and entertainers 'to be part of a culturally unique program' allowing them to teach or be part of festivals, workshops and conferences.[19] Artists need an invitation by a U.S. employer or sponsor for this type of visa and so students help by organizing workshops, inviting the artists and navigating the bureaucratic process of the application. Similar types of visas exist in other countries and a broadly circulating narrative, grounded in a few concrete examples, is that once performers are abroad, they abandon their dance troupe, leaving the artistic director without a group. Discussed in detail by Neveu Kringelbach (2005), this narrative is so widespread that it becomes a strong incentive for young Senegalese to join dance troupes and train hard in the hope that one day they will escape poverty. However, artists' ability to visit their home countries is restricted if they overstay their visas.

Another way for artists to travel abroad has been relationships with U.S. and other nationals. Some view marriage as the main way that dances have been exported internationally. A Senegalese *griot* for example told me that Sabar classes are typically set up by foreign students, who travel to Senegal, fall in love with Senegalese men, marry them and 'bring' them abroad to open dance centres. In his view, this is triggered by Westerners' unique obsession for the 'authentic', which brings them to West Africa to learn the dances 'at the root'. This description took on flesh and bones during my fieldwork through many stories of foreign women marrying West African men that extended beyond the dance community.[20] 'Falling in love with an African' is a ubiquitous stereotype that American women reflect on jokingly. However, it does not discourage them from engaging in similar relationships. In contrast, the narrative connecting foreign men and Senegalese women that circulated in Dakar amongst expats and Senegalese revolved around sex tourism and not love and marriage. Anthropological literature has focused almost exclusively on 'sex tourism' (Hall and Ryan 2001, Oppermann 1999, Seabrook 1996, Truong 1990 and Ebron 2002). Herold, Garcia and DeMoya (2001) while arguing against a polarized conception of tourist/local relationships as either sex tourism or romance, nevertheless maintain that most male tourist relationships in the Caribbean were placed towards the sex-tourism end of the spectrum while most female tourist relationships were towards the romance end.

Marrying someone from West Africa under current U.S. immigration laws is not easy and requires much time and effort. For example, Amy waited many years before she could move to the U.S. with her husband. During that period, she lived in Guinea where between the immigration paperwork and her full-time job she had no time to dance. Not everyone shares Amy's story. As different visa routes have different timeframes some applicants are luckier, or more informed, than others. 'Undiscovered' routes are faster in processing applications than the popular ones. But as those 'undiscovered' routes become popular they receive increasing applications and so gradually slow down. Alternative routes are then pursued. Stories of marriage are very common, but so are stories of divorce. Laura, a U.S. dancer, told me that out of the twelve couples she knew only one was still happily married. In most cases the men are 'taken out of Africa' and live a luxurious life in Europe or the U.S., but the marriage fails as 'African men are unfaithful', a commonly recited phrase amongst expats in Dakar. 'Cultural differences' was a Senegalese man's view of his divorce, after which he remained in the U.S. working in a full-time job while occasionally also teaching dance.

The widespread narratives of infidelity and divorce were familiar to many women I met who were in relationships with West African men. Similarly, many of them, albeit to different degrees, were conscious of the complexity of their relationships, and their unequal positions with their husbands in terms of their socio-economic status and possibilities for mobility in the world. In the following section I will broadly sketch out the two different narratives of marriage of the American women and the West African men, which, while somewhat stereotypical, nevertheless suggest an indicative framework for understanding these relationships.[21] As I illustrate later, participants have very different and often profound understandings of their involvement. As I was better positioned to discuss these relationships with the American women than the West African men, the following two narratives are uneven and reflect this imbalance in accessibility.

Weaving Narratives into Relationships

The story that leads American women to marriage is very different from that of the West African men. Marriage for the former is the result of a relationship based on love. As construed in romance films, the search for love involves a long search for someone understanding, caring and supportive. Relationships require mutual respect and a great investment of time and effort. The West African man brings another parameter into the relationship. He fits the role of 'the significant Other'. He is a drummer or a dancer, two 'truly African' occupations, and belongs to a world that is the extreme opposite to that of the American woman. As imagined, and lived, his world is more humane, simple, communal:

> I was received very openly . . . His family is great! Guineans are so warm. They have a very hospitable culture and ideas. I mean when you come in, everyone greets you. They offer you water if they have money, and everyone in the vicinity gets invited to eat . . . But you know its complex . . . (Penny, Dakar, 2007)

The hospitality can make one feel very special. His world is poor and perhaps invites a philanthropic response. An American woman's ability to help him and his family may satisfy a guilt nurtured by Hollywood movies, media headlines and NGO campaigns.

The West African man also makes her feel very special. He shows her Senegalese hospitality, *teranga*, which is marketed so well by his country. He brings her to his family, takes her to Gorée Island and protects her from the hassle of vendors. He appears sensitive and attentive.[22] He does not have 'commitment issues' and asks if she is married right away. She later discovers marriage does not have similar connotations in his culture. She is powerful in the relationship, feels special and loved, and is needed to help impoverished 'Others'. He serves as evidence of her politically correct stance and her open-mindedness, all positive moral qualities in her world. The story for the West African man is slightly different. He might be curious, enchanted by this woman's world. She can afford things. Association with her brings him prestige in the eyes of friends and family, and gives him access to venues reserved for the rich Senegalese. It would be very difficult to marry or even court a Senegalese woman of comparable wealth. And she's nice! – young and curvy, not skinny, like most *toubaabs* . . . She has light skin and will give him mixed children, like his friends in Europe or like President Wade![23] Maybe he can marry her and go to her country, and from there send money back to his family. He is lucky to have found this *toubaab*. Some of his friends have married older women – like his friend Modou. But Modou is lucky. He is already in Europe.

The two narratives of marriage enter into a relationship with the imagined world (Appadurai 1991) of the Other. The expectations from these narratives and imaginings of the Other are at times fulfilled by how the relationships unravel on the ground – at least at first. For example, the men's socio-economic mobility is transformed to that of the local elite and the *toubaabs*. On the other hand, marrying someone older is not what Senegalese men typically do. They choose wives younger than them, with the second wife expected to be younger than the first. Even Youssou NDour, the Senegalese pop star and until recently an exemplar of Wolof morality, was criticized for leaving his wife for someone older. An exception to this, I was told by my Wolof teacher, was Prophet Mohammed himself, whose first wife Kadija was much older than him. Her old age was counterbalanced by the fact that she was rich, suggesting perhaps similar incentives for the Senegalese men.

As relationships unravel, some women realize they have different expectations from marriage than their partners and so in contrast to Castaldi (2006), not all women I met were ignorant of the complexities in their relationships. They did not simply consume the Other, or what they believed the Other to be. Instead, there were different degrees of involvement and awareness which often depended on how long they had spent with their partners in Africa, how reflexive and critical they were of their situation and how involved they had chosen to be with their husbands' world. Those fluent in their husband's language, for example, had a more nuanced understanding of the power dynamics of their relationships than the women who did not share their husband's native language. As Amy explained, 'the face they present to foreigners and what they say amongst themselves is not always the same'. Thus the relationships are not founded merely on a consumption of the Other but become constant negotiations and compromises between the two narratives of marriage and imagining of the Other. Pruitt and LaFont (2001), in analysing 'romance' and 'love' relationships between American women and Jamaican men, argue that the relationships initially provide both sides with an opportunity to negotiate their gender identities as constructed in their respective societies. While at first the relationship appears to provide a *tabula rasa* upon which the partners can affirm their power over the other, free from the restraints of their respective societies, they soon realize that they are restrained by the parameters imposed by their partners:

> The dynamics of these relationships also demonstrate that dominance and power are not static, but are shifting and situational, constantly negotiated and contested. As the partners in these relationships play off traditional social and gender repertoires, as well as the immediate circumstances of finance and cultural capital, the power in the relationship fluctuates between them 'in relation to opposed sets of cultural values and established social boundaries'. (Conway, Bourque and Scott, in Pruitt and LaFont 2001: 437)

An added parameter here is that participants know very well the failures of similar relationships. Not all men marry and travel abroad, and many women are well familiar with stories of divorce from their immediate circle of friends. Yet, the example set by the few relationships 'that work' where the man 'was taken out of Africa' function as examples for others. They become imaginative possibilities, encouraging both sides to engage in similar endeavours.

Crossing Back Over to the USA

Once in the U.S., new dancers and drummers receive help from older migrants, U.S. students, friends, partners and spouses in setting up classes and maintaining a regular income. Once established as a teacher, a dancer can also organize trips abroad. Friends, students and spouses help by writing and promoting the brochures:

> This blog is mainly written by me, Abdoulaye's wife, Julia . . . This will be a real taste of Africa, providing you with a deeper and more authentic understanding of African life than you would get from an

air-conditioned hotel room . . . Attend a farewell party in your honor, given by Abdoulaye's family! . . . Instructors will be sure to provide challenge for experienced drummers and dancers while supporting beginners in learning the basics. This trip is designed for flexible people with a spirit of adventure and a sincere desire to see the real Senegal.

The fact that these brochures are written by American women adds another layer to these representations. The romantic image of Africa is promoted as an established attraction to new students by West African men and their U.S. partners, thus complicating further the idea of the consuming West and the consumed Africa. Relations between Africa and the West can no longer be understood as a dichotomist structure of exploitation, as the following quote suggests:

> Representations of the African were, and are, evidently not 'fixed' but eminently recuperable and variable, depending on the political exigencies of any specific historical conjuncture. As such, they necessarily tell us more about the nexus of European interests in African affairs and about the coloniser than they do about Africa and the African over this period. (Coombes 1994: 3)

Rather, the relationship between American women and West African men is one of partnership, which invites a third actor, the new student of West African dance. In this way 'the agency has shifted from the characteristic nation-state and its trans-national corporations to the intimately personal arena' (Pruitt and LaFont 2001: 438), rendering national definitions of actors irrelevant. In the 'intimately personal arena' of transatlantic relationships, the West African man and the American woman stand against the new student of West African dance. In one sense, the couple is in charge of the relationship with the student, as they choose what romantic image of Africa to promote. At a closer look, however, the new student also has power, as the couple needs to choose a 'context' that resonates with her. In this setting knowledge translates to power in the sense that the couple, knowing what sells, can profit from it. Power however also lies with the 'not-knowing' student, whose imagination of 'Africa' essentially dictates what kind of 'context' she is willing to consume. It thus becomes difficult to assign power when asking who defines this interaction.

Finally, the position of actors in this process is not fixed but shifting. The student who will soon be attracted to travel to West Africa may engage in a romantic relationship with a West African man. She may move back to the United States with her partner or spouse and in the future may write brochures advertising her husband's trips to West Africa. As such she will be translating and promoting her husband's culture to future new students, essentially feeding back to new students those first images that attracted her to Africa. Thus actors' understandings and positionalities also shift over time. The fact that the romantic version of Africa is employed strategically in this process emphasizes the importance of looking at who produces these images, who consumes them and how they consume them when choosing to analyse representations. Here the attraction of the romantic Africa often leads to a longer involvement with the place and eventually the student's nuanced understanding of the specificities, power dynamics and complex realities of West African countries.

Notes

1. From 2006 to 2008 the cost of the trips ranged from $400.00 to $500.00 (U.S.) per week, depending on the reputation of the teacher. The cost included accommodation, meals, dance and drum classes, attending cultural events and ceremonies, and trips to the market and rural areas. The airfare of $1,000.00 to $2,000.00 was extra. For students who embarked on trips on their own there were networks in West Africa of West Africans and Americans to accommodate the demand.

2. Laura was in her mid-thirties and was introduced to the dances while living on the West Coast of the U.S. She described those classes as promoting healing and well-being through dance.

3. Mary, 45, has been a long-term dancer of Djembé. We met in Dakar where Mary was visiting a friend, another Djembé student, on her way to Mali. Both women were active in organizing workshops in the U.S. and in inviting guest teachers from West Africa.

4. June, in her early thirties, described herself as white from a Jewish background. She had worked as a Peace Corp volunteer in East Africa and travelled widely in Africa. She had been introduced to West African dances as an undergraduate student at a U.S. university, and considered West African dance to be a top priority in her life.

5. Gorée Island is off the coast of Dakar. A historical and UNESCO World Heritage site, Gorée was the largest slave-trading centre on the African coast and is visited by many tourists every year, especially African Americans.

6. I do not provide the names of any of the websites as that would identify the individuals involved and because they are of no significance to my analysis other than the common themes of the advertisements.

7. Emailed to AfricanDance_New York on 31 December 2006.

8. Emailed to AfricanDance_New York on 26 October 2007.

9. Retrieved from website on 14 February 2008.

10. Retrieved from website on 25 January 2008.

11. Email to AfricanDance_New York on 8 August 2006.

12. It is difficult to ignore the echoes of anthropological methodology here. Ebron (2002) argues that experience and the everyday have been prominent themes in anthropological works on Africa.

13. *Ceebujen* is a traditional dish of fish with rice, and also the name of a Sabar dance-rhythm.

14. Ann-Sophie was in her late twenties and had previously spent two years studying Sabar in Senegal. She complemented her practice of Sabar with independent research, which she abandoned, she explained, because of the contradictory information she had received. She visited West Africa often to also develop her knowledge and practice of Djembé. As a

professional dancer she aimed to synthesize her modern dance training with West African dances.

15. On this line Frankland argues that Turnbull's 1983 analysis of the pygmies in Mount Hoyo concludes that 'the contaminated can only be the fake other' (Frankland 2001: 246).

16. These students are like tourists in that they approach their travelling as a very personal endeavour, claiming often explicitly that they wish to change, define or negotiate who they are. While there are arguments on this line by many scholars of tourism (MacCannell 1976, Munt 1994, Urry 1995, Desforges 2000), I do not think they are helpful in understanding the reasons for these participants' travels to West Africa. This is because they travel due to their engagement with the dances, and these engagements often turn into lifelong affairs.

17. *Doudounbas* in Guinea are organized for various occasions and require funding for the fees of the drummers and the setting up of the event, for example to rent chairs.

18. While U.S. and EU citizens ought to leave the country within three months of entry, most visitors did not have difficulty acquiring visas for longer periods, even in situ.

19. U.S. Citizenship and Immigration Services, www.uscis.gov, on 31 January 2011.

20. An illustrative example is when I once asked after Karen's friend, who I described as 'married to a Guinean'; she went through four names before we found the woman in question. While it is hard to provide figures, an indication of the large numbers involved are the emails sent by the U.S. embassy in Dakar to registered Americans informing them of which kind of marriages are recognized by the U.S. government. The importance of this email and its broad relevance are indicated by the fact that all other emails from the U.S. embassy in Dakar concerned security issues.

21. Castaldi (2006) in her chapter 'Tales of Betrayal' provides very evocative perspectives on the interaction and power dynamics between 'white' women, 'black' women and 'black' men. From an earlier period, Fanon offers a different view of these relationships (Fanon [1952] 1986).

22. Women often contrasted this public persona of sensitivity and care with their surprise at what they described as 'lack of sensitivity' and selfishness of their African partners in the intimate arena.

23. Two of the three former presidents of Senegal were married to white French women: Léopold Sédar Senghor (1960–1980) and Abdoulaye Wade (2001–2012).

Chapter 4

Re-choreographing Sabar

The 'context' of Djembé and Sabar is complicated further in West Africa as the forms are taught in different environments. This chapter focuses on Dakar and explores how different forms of Sabar are produced in different learning contexts: Sabar taught to international students, Sabar as performed in street-Sabars and Sabar as learned in a *géwël* household. These different settings are not distinct, as dancers and movements circulate through all. However, they are different in the pedagogical techniques used and, consequently, in the forms of Sabar they envelop and produce. The chapter will explore how these forms are understood, reproduced and contested by dancers positioned differently in the Dakar sphere of dance genres.

'Traditional Dances' for International Students

Local professionals in Dakar cater to the international demand for West African dances.[1] Traditional dances are often taught along with 'context' and are often included in 'cultural trips' with activities such as going to the market, learning to cook and learning to speak Wolof. Lessons to foreigners have common themes in their content and structure, which are adjusted to international students' aesthetics and expectations. However, certain aesthetics and social norms resist. In this chapter I explore this negotiation and how it is reflected in the pedagogical techniques and consequently the forms of Sabar they produce.

I arranged my first lessons in Dakar with Ousmane, the manager of a traditional ballet who was introduced to me as an authority on the dances. Ousmane's wife Fatou was to be my teacher for the next month. Fatou was a beautiful woman, adhering well to Senegalese aesthetic standards, with a full curvy figure and beautifully matched outfits; 'In Europe you look at women in the eyes, here we look at the ass', a Senegalese artist once told me jokingly. My lessons were at the Centre Culturel Blaise Senghor (CCBS), a very busy complex of performance spaces hosting classes and daily ballet rehearsals. My classes took place on a concrete block surrounded by unkempt bushes and trees embellished with black plastic bags, cups and empty snack wrappings. Three goatskins were drying in the sun to be later fitted onto Sabar drums. The odour of the skins, encouraged by the sun, saturated my learning. While walking next to Fatou on that first day she stepped on some broken glass: 'My feet are my living' she mumbled, while picking out the pieces.

Traditional West African dance classes are an established commodity. Their structure is adjusted to the market of international students and promoted through a Euro-American 'business' framework. Ousmane for example insisted on establishing the number and duration of my lessons; we negotiated a price and he offered to keep a written record of our agreement.[2] I was not able to record the lessons, as in the past a *toubaab* had paid 200,000 CFA (about £200) to record the dances of Ousmane's dance company; and while I explained that I was not interested in reproducing or showing the choreographies but only in keeping a record of my dancing (the camera would be pointing at me) I was refused on the grounds that the rhythm belongs to the drummer. The promised structure of the lessons however contrasted strongly with the way the classes unfolded. The teacher and drummer were often late, and at times did not show up or interrupted the lessons to buy from passer-by vendors. Events like this often lead to discontent from international students who interpret them as 'lack of professionalism'. The promised professionalism of the classes is also negotiated with local expectations placed on social ties and gender roles. So when the drummer was late, an infuriated Fatou would complain that 'he is not professional!' However, she never confronted him, as the drummer is a man and her husband's friend. The drummer was not appointed because of his drumming skills but rather because he had a family and was unemployed. In fact, the drummer learned the rhythms as the lessons progressed. Thus the attempted 'business' structure of lessons for international students is negotiated with the expectations and restraints imposed by traditional social roles.

The commoditization of the dances has lead to the standardization of lessons for foreigners. The lessons provide a repertoire of 'traditional' movements that are structured in choreographies similar to ballet performances. In that way they resemble New York classes. Certain dances and movements are preferred over others, but the lessons have a common structure and use similar teaching techniques. Fatou's classes, like New York classes, started with a warm-up. The movements were taught 'broken down', and were arranged in a longer choreography expected to be performed in that order. Learning how to improvise was not an objective of our lesson, even if improvisation is a very important aesthetic in Sabar, as discussed below. Foreigners are taught what is thought to sell internationally, and the international success of traditional ballets means that teachers borrow from ballet performances and mostly teach Djembé. So Fatou first taught me a Djembé dance from Mali called *lamban*, a favourite of international students and New York classes. Fatou asked me to show her what I had learned in New York and then commented that the moves I knew were 'old' and not interesting. 'New' movements are preferred to 'old', and so teaching the latest moves increases the value of the lessons. U.S. students with a long experience in West Africa share this understanding. However, the movements of the dance may be 'new' but they are still 'traditional' as they come from the repertoire of ballets, similar to the choreographies taught in New York. Thus while *lamban* is described as a 'traditional' dance, it does not resist innovation.

Teachers may accommodate the demands of foreign students but in many ways their demands are resisted. For example, Fatou first started teaching me traditional Sabar dances like *dagagni*, which I never saw performed in street-Sabars. We then moved to more popular dance-rhythms like *baar mbaye, farwu jar* and *ceebujen*. We had decided not to do *yabba*, a dance for 'older women' and *lëmbël*. *Lëmbël* is not part of the usual repertoire taught to foreigners even though it was perhaps the dance I saw performed most often in street-Sabars, videos and nightclubs. Fatou explained that while she had danced *lëmbël* before she got married, she no longer liked it. She found it inappropriate for married women and refused to teach me. When I protested, explaining that I had seen it many times and would like to learn it, she replied that I had seen it because prostitutes use the sensual movements of the dance to enchant foreign businessmen and tourists. This indicates the different moral values attached to the different dance-rhythms and how this depends on the position of the dancer within the field of dance genres in Dakar. So even though Fatou refused to teach me *lëmbël*, I was able to learn it from another teacher – a dancer whose dancing caters to domestic consumption.

Teachers like Fatou are chosen for their knowledge of 'traditional' dances, grounded on their training and performance with traditional and folkloric ballets. Beyond representing their countries and dances on stage, these dancers promote a certain kind of Sabar when teaching international students. However the themes of ballet performances vary greatly depending on how the ballet and the artistic director position themselves in the local and global artistic scene, as well as in relation to the local tourism industry. It is not the place here to discuss in detail the historical emergence of ballets, their relation to different ethnic traditions and their position in Dakar and abroad, which has been excellently addressed by previous studies (Castaldi 2006, Neveu Kringelbach 2005). However, I will aim to give the reader an understanding of the diversity of ballet performances and the way they are positioned in the Dakarois dance sphere in order to better situate the lessons to foreigners against the different learning setting of the *géwël* household.

Traditional and Folkloric Ballets

Forêt Sacrée (Sacred Forest) is a folkloric ballet, whose artistic director is from Guinea. The dancers and drummers are Senegalese in the majority, and the ballet performs mostly Djembé. The following description is taken from their performance at a luxury hotel in Dakar for the 2007 Lisbon–Dakar Rally:

> I arrive at Casino Terrou-Bi and enter a sound-scape of African MTV hits: the late Cape Verdean singer Cesária Évora and Youssou NDour's 1990s hit 'Seven Seconds Away'. The audience is European and tanned, mostly male. The event has a scent of after-sun products. I pick out English, Portuguese, French and Spanish. A Brazilian employee of the oil and gas company Total tells me they handed out trucks of toys to children in Saly the day before and, as he expects, I respond by praising his charitable actions. I leave to find the dancers who are changing in a makeshift closed-off area behind the buffet. They are slipping into their Senegalese flag outfits. The artistic director is prepping the dancers: 'you have to dance *lëmbël* well!' As a provocative dance, *lëmbël* is expected to bring the dancers more tips from this predominantly male audience. The performance is adjusted to the setting of the hotel and the buffet; the drummers are set by the pool and the dancers dance between the buffet and the tables. The performance begins with Djembé, and a male dancer enters the 'stage' in summersaults, bare-chested, wearing animal skins for a skirt and clenching a branch of leaves in his teeth. More dancers follow, wearing big masks and furry outfits, jumping in seemingly unstructured ways. They are supposed to be animals and the bare-chested dancer is hunting them, aiming at them with his invisible spear. (Edited Field Notes, 20 January 2007)

Forêt Sacrée performs mostly in tourist settings, and their performances often evoke themes of a rural, African village, and stories of hunting and witchcraft. This is an instrumental choice in an attempt to evoke a specific Africa of tradition and authenticity used by traditional ballets more broadly. Castaldi argues that the National Ballet of Senegal 'cashes in on these assumptions and is able to commodify "purity" at a higher price than "contaminated" representation of African dance would allow' (Castaldi 2006: 68). In contrast, Sabar and its popular dance form Mbalax found in the urban setting of Dakar and disseminated through the media can be considered relics of Western influence that challenge ideas of a traditional dance (Castaldi 2006).

However, as Neveu Kringelbach argues, folkloric performances are not solely aimed at international marketing but are instead adjusted and adapted to the performers' own agendas so as to resonate with the different audiences:

> Many Senegalese folkloric troupes . . . are equally able to embody ethnic identities for events organized by local associations, project the image of Senegal as a united nation or construct representations of 'traditional Africa' for tourists. (Neveu Kringelbach 2005: 104)

Some ballets for example may also address topics that are thought to attract funding from NGOs and charities, but this 'political dimension of folkloric performance as "imagined tradition" should not obscure the fact that it helps maintain an idea of "home" for many urban migrants and their children' (Neveu Kringelbach 2005: 196). Performances may also be used to locate and promote oneself in relation to Euro-American categories of art and current international debates. For example the performance of a *Semi-Folkloric* ballet during the bi-annual international dance festival in Dakar, 'Kaay Fecc' (Come Dance!), was set in a rural community in southern Senegal and portrayed the emancipation of women who revolted against their husbands for their unequal workload. The dance troupe used the opportunity to perform in an international event to locate itself within Euro-American feminist debates.

Thus dancers and dance troupes negotiate many agendas at any time, an example of which was presented to me during two different interviews with the same dancer. On the two different occasions I received contradictory responses when I enquired about the relationship between traditional Senegalese conceptions of 'caste' and dance. In the first instance, from the role of a contemporary artist, the dancer criticized the negative connotations that have traditionally accompanied 'caste' and dance in Senegal. On the second occasion, seven months later, the artist negated the existence of such negative perceptions, this time from the role of an organizer of an international workshop representing the Senegalese artistic scene to a foreigner. Dance in Senegal thus continues to act as a means of representation. The instrumental use of ballet performances in the 1960s is perpetuated today, albeit for different reasons and adjusted to a contemporary setting. This in turn affects how the dances are commoditized and promoted to foreign students. Students prefer dancers from ballets for their knowledge of traditional dances, grounded on an understanding of tradition as distinct from what is observable in the social dance sphere of Dakar.

Learning in a *Géwël* Household

When Ashtou, a *géwël* dancer, asked me to show her what I had learned from my previous teacher, I danced a short choreography of the dance-rhythm *ceebujen*. Ashtou was confused. If I performed this in front of drummers, she said, they would not know what I was doing. What Fatou had taught me, she said, was not *ceebujen* but *ceebujen* mixed with ballet. This meant that the movements were structured for a ballet performance as opposed to the way movements are combined when performing in Sabar-events. This difference is significant because it essentially denotes two distinct forms of dance. Choreographies from ballet teachers cannot be performed in Sabar-events. On the other hand ballet dancers often talk of the dancing in Sabar-events as technically inferior. I will explore the significance of these differences following the introduction of another learning context of Sabar, the *géwël* household.

Ashtou's House

> When you go to Senegal, don't go to a centre to learn, go to a family, because a family . . . that's where the real deal is, the centre they're learning like you. Why you want to go to some people who learned it? You gotta go to some original roots, like the house that is *griot* . . . (*Géwël* dancer, New York, July 2008)

During the first months in Senegal, I trained mostly with dancers experienced in teaching foreigners. Curious to discover what was popular locally, I was referred to Ashtou, a dancer in popular television Mbalax videos. Ashtou was twenty-two and had been dancing in Mbalax videos for the last three years. She was very successful, appearing in the videos of the most popular Senegalese artists. Ashtou was a very beautiful woman, with a full and curvy figure. Her dress style was impeccable, always dressing in elegant, matching outfits. She would switch between *traditionnel* ('African') and *moderne* (Western) outfits, staying true to the style in the choice of accessories. In the characteristic Senegalese aesthetic, she matched complementary bright colours in clothes to her make-up and accessories in the same colour scheme. Her hair was braided or covered under wigs, which were always new and combed, and never worn once too entangled.

Ashtou's house was in Pikine, a poor district on the outskirts of Dakar. Her room was on the top floor of a two-storey building. There were four rooms on each floor, all with a large bed, a few suitcases on top of a wardrobe and a big coloured television. The complex housed Ashtou's extended family, and slept around four people per bed. They shared the upstairs toilet and the ground floor cooking area with a fridge in the enclosed courtyard. The walls of the courtyard were worn out and inscribed with telephone numbers detached from any names they might belong to. Broken mirror pieces were screwed on the wall, where women would gather to apply their make-up. Colourful clothes would be hung to dry in the courtyard, which was full of children, friends and neighbours, as women chatted and gossiped over cooking and ironing. Outside the complex were the sandy streets that are so typical of Dakar. Ashtou's grandmother kept a stand there, from where she sold Senegalese snacks and seasonal fruit, a characteristic initiative by Senegalese women to maintain their own income. She was not required to watch the stand constantly, as any neighbours or family members who were hanging around would always help potential customers. The women would wash clothes in big colourful buckets in the middle of the street, while children played on the side. When finished, they would toss the water on the sand, awakening hidden, uncomfortable smells. Pikine's sounds, smells and colours are overwhelming to the senses of a *toubaab*.

People drifted in and out of the walls of the complex throughout the day. Visits declare amicable feelings for the hosts, and so frequent visits and phone calls, if unable to visit, are very important in Senegal. Youssou NDour's 2007 hit song 'Telephonbi' [The telephone] illustrates this:

> Just because we have telephones it doesn't mean that we are not obliged to see each other. Because in our tradition everything is, everyone is here under the tree [we do everything together] and people talk about their problems. If we don't solve the problems, the next day we try again. The telephone is here but we are obliged to meet. (Loose translation from Wolof by Tony Diamanka, Dakar, 2007)

With the exception of Ashtou's husband who could afford to visit regularly, men were largely absent from the household. Ashtou's father was in Italy and her uncle in Australia, both working as drummers. Ashtou's husband travelled abroad regularly with his dance company. The husbands' presence in the house was mostly evinced through the phone calls, gifts, and the children. When I once asked Ashtou's cousin where all the men were she replied, giggling, 'they are away, they work, and we stay home and make ourselves pretty'.

As drumming and dancing are traditionally a 'caste' occupation of the *géwël*, when a family has many musicians and dancers, one can safely assume that the family is *géwël*. Ashtou often denied this, whereas her aunt asserted it in an effort to explain the great grandmother's frequent requests for money. 'Persistent begging is one of the most common signs by which they [the *géwël*] are known' (Wright 1989: 50).[3]

Learning from Mbalax Clips

Television dominates in many Senegalese households. In my case this was accentuated by the fact that my teachers tried to accommodate my interest to learn. We would spend a typical day with Ashtou in her room watching Mbalax clips on television or DVDs from Sabar-events she had attended.[4] People would enter and leave the room, borrow clothes, try on make-up, ask for money, braid each other's hair or simply say hello. My learning how to dance, like the cooking, washing, and the children's homework, was treated as any other activity that 'had to be done' and so was shared between 'the people of the house' as the Wolof say to include those living in the same household (*keur*) at any one time. Anyone who happened to pass by would volunteer an instruction: 'You have to really smile!' or 'Hélène, come dance!'

One of the first things Ashtou taught me was Mbaye Ndieye Faye's 'Blokas'. Blokas was a Mbalax hit that dominated the Senegalese sound-scape in 2007, until it was replaced by hits from Youssou NDour's new album 'Alasaama Day'. Blokas was on the radio, on television, in cyber cafés, taxis and *car rapides* (small buses). It was played in nightclubs and was my teacher's ringtone. Similar to the song, the movements of the video travelled through many dancers. I saw Blokas by twelve-year-olds on the beach, by Senegalese women seducing expats in nightclubs, by older women at private dance-events and by twenty-year-olds on a night out. A year and a half later, transcending the boundaries of Senegal, I was taught Blokas in a New York class. Blokas is what Ashtou thought I should learn first. I was taught the movement that reappeared in the video at the end of a musical phrase: bent knees and the slow opening and closing of one's legs like butterfly wings while slowly tilting one's hips to alternate sides, and gradually lowering the hips to the floor. The arms moved in a rowing-like motion, and at the end of the movement, as signalled by a double drum stroke, the legs open outwards in two beats while the arms move as if pulling a string placed in front of the dancer – right arm moving up while the left moved down. The movements preceding and following this 'key' movement were also important. Some of these annotated the lyrics, so when the singer said *khol ko* (look at it), the dancers in the video placed their right hands on their foreheads as if trying to locate something at a distance, while leaning forward to the beat of two drum strokes.

Copying movements from Mbalax videos is very common. Dancers joke that there is a new choreography out every couple of weeks. The movements are introduced through videos and the private setting of one's home to be later taken up and performed in more public spaces: night clubs and dance-events in Dakar's neighbourhoods. Depending on the popularity of these choreographies, some will stay around longer than others. For example the *lëmbël* movement 'le ventilateur' still danced today can be traced back to 1982 (Duran 1989). The choreography of the video is not simply transmitted and performed as a set combination of movements. The videos do not determine what will be danced in the social domain but rather provide the grounds for further improvisation. They do so by popularizing the rhythmic phrase of the choreography. This rhythmic phrase is then used as the grounds for improvisation by both lay and professional dancers in private and public settings. To show how this works I will describe the learning setting at my teacher's house. In Ashtou's room, we imitated movements from videos, often joined by her friends and cousins. We would not simply copy the movements. Instead someone would introduce a variation on a certain move and the rest of us would pick it up and dance it until a new movement was introduced. This imitation and exchange of movements with others, which I call 'creative imitation', is an important aspect of dancing Sabar, as I will discuss in detail in the next chapters. It helps dancers to build a repertoire of movements, and the knowledge of what movements are similar to others and thus interchangeable. This knowledge is then used to spice up one's solo performance in Sabar-events.

A similar process takes place in public events. In Sabar-events the drummers play familiar rhythmic phrases, called *bàkk*s. These *bàkk*s come from different sources and may be the drummers' creations or popular Mbalax hits. The drummers overlay *bàkk*s on Sabar rhythms (such as *baar mbaye* or *ceebujen*) and play them repeatedly, inviting the audience members one by one to enter the circle and perform a short solo. The dancer's solo is guided by the *bàkk* as the movements correspond to the accompanying drum strokes. The solo is also creative, however, as the dancer can choose what movements to combine. Thus the *bàkk* does not determine but rather guides the dancer's solo. The choice of movements lies with the dancer and is grounded on the knowledge of what movements are similar and thus interchangeable.

While lay dancers almost always remain faithful to the rhythmic structure of the *bàkk*, professional dancers may improvise further. They will stretch out the rhythmic structure or introduce new elements by guiding the drummers with their movements. As professional dancers form the link between videos and the public sphere, if a certain improvisation is good, it may be picked up and performed in a video:

> People take movements from videos to the street . . . and then people dance in the street, make it nice, take it to videos . . . and you see it again in video, you're like 'Wow, this is hot! Let me get it!' (Sabar teacher, New York, 2008)

These new improvisations or *créations* will then become popular and inspire new *créations* for future videos.[5] Thus the dancing 'captured' in the video clips is not approached as a set combination of movements to be imitated, but the movements provide the grounds for further improvisation. Videos are then appropriated according to the local dance aesthetic that values the dancer's ability to improvise. Mbalax videos stand in a dialectic relationship to the dancing of the private and the public spheres of Dakar, and can be seen as one part of a larger process through which dance movements circulate and transform.

Television: A New Domain for Dance

Television Mbalax videos, however, also introduce a new learning setting – one's home – and in doing so challenge traditional social roles. In contrast to the traditional and 'formalized' learning settings for professional dancers – the *géwël* household, dance schools and ballets – lay dancers learn informally. Public performances provide an opportunity for children to imitate adults and experiment with their dancing. Mbalax videos delineate a new context for learning that allows indiscriminate accessibility to anyone who wishes to learn; this, however, is seen by some to be a shift from 'tradition'. In the words of drummer Babacar:

> We have lost what was natural. The children no longer have the opportunity to learn to dance in public, in a Sabar organized in the *quartiers* (districts, neighbourhoods) where everyone, the mothers get together. The problem today is that children learn in the house, in front of the TV, the mom beats [the rhythm], they dance. They dance in front of the TV, in front of their parents . . . and there is something missing. (Babacar, Dakar, 2006)

Videos may be a negative development for Babacar, but the new private setting they introduce helps to transcend conventional notions of who can dance. The significance of this is great, as the appropriateness of someone's dancing is negotiated by one's age, gender, 'caste' and the privacy of the performance setting (Irvine 1974: 303). Sabar 'dancing is recontextualized repeatedly over the course of an individual's life as she or he moves from childhood to maturity and in and out of settings where particular ideological orientations and social relations are salient' (Heath 1994: 92).[6] As such, older, married *géer* women will avoid dancing in public events organized in the streets that are accessible to an indiscriminate audience. They can, however, dance in exclusively female private events. For example, my Wolof teacher, a married, religious woman, had long abandoned dancing in street Sabars, as she did not view them as being appropriate for her role as a wife and a fervent Muslim. She did, however, dance at home with the children 'in front of the TV'. So it was not the actual dancing that conflicted with her social and religious status, but the act of doing it in public. Mbalax videos allowed her to circumvent her social and religious commitments by providing a private space for her to dance. Thus for many, the new learning setting of their private home allows freedoms they could not access otherwise.

In contrast to the ephemeral nature of Sabar-events that limit the dancing to the audience present at a particular time, recorded performances have a 'set' quality.[7] This has led to confusing dance contexts and challenging social norms and propriety. An example was the scandal *Gùddi Town* that made the Senegalese media headlines in 2007 and involved a recorded performance from a nightclub. An audience member captured the performance of the sensual dance-rhythm *lëmbël* that was performed for a competition organized in the club. The video was never broadcasted on television but made its way into people's homes through the internet and through pirate copies sold in Dakar's markets. *Lëmbël* is widely performed in Senegal and is usually the last rhythm in a street Sabar-event. However *lëmbël* movements vary in degrees of sensuality. The more explicit movements are said to be reserved for the bedroom and one's husband. They are also found in private, exclusively female events. In contrast, *lëmbël* on Mbalax clips is more restrained. This limits provocative *lëmbël* movements to specific audiences and occasions.

The *Gùddi Town* recording challenged this by making the explicit dancing of the event available to those who were not present. In the controversy that surrounded the video, religious authorities and conservative views condemned the video and the dancers for corruption of morals. Those on the more liberal side noted the scandal's hypocrisy, as *lëmbël* is performed widely and everyone is well aware of it. Following the scandal, rumours circulated that one dancer's husband filed for divorce while another dancer's parents funded her move to Europe. The dimension of the scandal is indicative of the ambiguous relationship of Sabar to Islam in Senegal (see Neveu Kringelbach 2005). Critiques of the dances as too sensual, which remain mostly silent, find expression in instances of shifting or ambiguous contexts. This emphasizes the importance of the performance setting as the ephemeral nature and restricted access to a Sabar-event is challenged by technology that makes a performance accessible to an indiscriminate audience.

Contesting the Dance

> Ashtou is good, but she only knows *musique* [Mbalax]. (Ballet dancer, Dakar, 2007)

Mbalax is also criticized for the quality of the dancing on the videos. These critiques come from ballet dancers as well as contemporary dancers who deem Mbalax dancing unworthy, provocative and a shift from 'tradition'. Former ballet dancer and current director, Abdou Ba, considers Mbalax dancing lazy; a result of youth's tendency to seek comfort. This discourages the rigorous study of traditional dances, he argues, and makes dancers unfit to teach foreigners. Abdou Ba opposed this to the 'ancestors' and advised me to observe the dancing of the elders – not the youth – in Sabar-events: 'It is there that you find the real traditional dance'. For Abdou Ba, Mbalax marks the end of an era of 'traditional' dance, which the past generation studied diligently to promote proudly to the world. Foreign students echo this view, perhaps because most of their teachers come from this training:

> When I talk about Sabar I think that there are traditional dances from the different ethnicities, the Lebu, the Walo, the Wolof . . . so there is a base of traditional dances, *baar mbaye, ceebujen, kaolack, mbabas*. Now the new dances we're talking about, *blokas, raas*, for me they are not Sabar. (French Sabar student, Dakar, 2007)

Mbalax is also considered licentious and is judged negatively for the sensuality of the movements:

Yeah, Blokas, is what? . . . It's to provoke . . . It's only movements of the pelvis, movements that suggest sexual movements. (Traditional ballet dancer, Dakar, 2007)

They derive from Sabar but for me they are the popular aspect . . . of the dance. That's often something that tarnishes, dulls, the image of dance, the image of Sabar, the image of women here in the Sabar. That's why you have such reactions when you discuss with Senegalese, especially men, and they say 'No, I don't go to Sabars because women go to show their bums there'. (French Sabar student, Dakar, 2007)

Mbalax is also criticized for the lack of time investment and creativity in choreographies:

I'm not happy with the clips because the youth doesn't make an effort to create. Often they tell them we'll do a clip, tomorrow you will come to dance, they take the music, they listen to it, they'll go dance. They don't work to create. I think that those who make the clips should be interested in taking real choreographers to give them the text of the clip and to give them the liberty to show real artistic creations. When that's not done we will have Sabar dance of third and fourth category [low quality]. (Contemporary dancer, Dakar, 2007)

Here, Mbalax is compared to other dance forms, and expectations are imposed on artistic authorship, creativity and competence that normally characterize traditional ballets or professional dance performances. Not all contemporary dancers share this view. In fact many simply do not consider Mbalax to be dance, arguing that its main function is to accompany the music and so dancing is there to 'entertain' and not for 'the dance's sake'.

At first, the distinction between traditional dance and today's popular 'unworthy' version seems to echo Western distinctions between popular and high art culture. Schulz makes a similar observation in her discussion of Malian music TV clips and their reception (Schulz 2001), arguing that the authority of the *Jeli* (griot) female singers is challenged by Malian intellectuals who write 'with nostalgia for an "authentic" tradition and feel deeply concerned about contemporary decay, corruption and the breakdown of deep-rooted traditions' (ibid.: 347). Following Barber (1987), Schulz argues against a reading of this as an echo of Western distinctions, and instead, aiming to locate its significance within the local discourses on 'modern life', she theorizes that the videos provide a variety of readings for the audiences that reconcile the dichotomy between the loss of moral values associated with an urban, modern life and the traditional 'authentic' ethics associated with life in the village. Similarly, Western categories of 'high' and 'popular' art seem inappropriate for Mbalax videos which are understood and valued differently, depending on the position of the professional and lay dancer in Dakar.

The neatly delineated views above do not characterize the majority of dancers who circulate between the different dance genres. In fact, many dancers approach the different genres for 'what they have to offer'. So while they may train in ballets for the knowledge of ethnic traditions and the opportunity for international travel, they may also stay up to date with the latest Mbalax *créations* so as to impress in street-Sabars. Essentially, 'pop' and 'traditional' meet on the dance floor.

Together on the Dance Floor

It's the same thing! Before it was the movements we did in the marriages that we would dance in the clips. Now it's the movements from the clips that go to the dances in the street. It's the consequence of the TV . . . it's now the clips that dictate the new dances. (Sabar teacher, New York, 2008)

The distinctions between 'traditional' Sabar and Mbalax are not as articulate on the dance floor. Street-Sabars will begin their repertoire with 'traditional' rhythms and end with the latest Mbalax hits. André below describes the sequence of dance-rhythms in a Sabar repertoire:

First of all, there is *ardin* [this rhythm is not danced], the warm-up before *farwu jar*. Original Sabar starts from *farwu jar*, then you go to *ceebujen*. After *baar mbaye*, then there is *kaolack*, then *mbabas*, which is the same as *niarigoron* but just faster . . . Usually after that they have *lëmbël*, or something like *blokas* – whatever is new they're gonna start dancing at that moment.[8]

Mbalax also affects the way movements are combined in public performances. The traditional format in Sabar-events is for dancers to step into the circle one by one, and perform short solos while facing the drummers. Other dancers may join the soloist and mirror her movements to express their appreciation for the dancing. However, it is not uncommon today for two or more professional dancers to perform prearranged choreographies while standing in alignment, in a form that resembles dancing in ballets, Mbalax and U.S. hip-hop videos.

Castaldi (2006) argues against dichotomies that oppose 'tradition' and 'authenticity' to the contemporary popular dancing of the urban sphere of Dakar (cf. Nicholls 1996). The two are interrelated, she argues, as movements and dancers circulate between both 'genres'. Ballet choreographies often include segments of Sabar, and Mbalax choreographies once performed on the street make their way onto the stage. While this is the case, the two settings also produce different forms of Sabar that invite contesting discourses from the differently situated actors in Dakar's dance-scape. More importantly, the two spheres translate into two different learning settings: the dance that caters to the international market and the dance consumed locally. The first is closer to the Sabar of traditional ballets where movements are arranged into longer choreographies, while the popular version Mbalax is appropriated for improvisation. The long history of the export of ballets, and the outside world's insistence for the 'authentic', means that teachers mainly borrow from ballets rather than from what is popular in Senegal when teaching foreigners. As such, foreigners are not taught how to improvise but rather how to memorize a series of movements for different dance-rhythms (*baar mbaye, ceebujen, farwu jar*, etc.). The difference produced by the two learning settings lies most importantly in the way movements are combined. The importance of this is highlighted when considering that novelty and creative authorship in Sabar is often dependent on how movements are combined and not necessarily on the movements themselves. Having discussed the socio-cultural setting of Sabar learning spaces in New York and Dakar, the following chapters will focus more closely on the pedagogical techniques and, consequently, the forms of Sabar that are produced in these settings.

Notes

1. During this fieldwork I met students from Europe, the U.S. and Japan travelling independently or in groups. Senegal was often the first stop in West Africa, to be followed by visits to Mali, Guinea or Ghana. Following their initial visit some students settled in Dakar. Dance is also included in tourist packages that offer the experience of the 'routine of African life'. Such packages arranged, for example, tourists' accommodation with families. Anticipating potential problems due to 'cultural differences', they also made alternative arrangements in hotels to provide customers with privacy, warm water and air conditioning.

2. Ousmane suggested the standard rate he gives to U.S. students, which he adjusted to my case as I was not American. I was told that 2,000 CFA (£2.00) out of the 6,000 CFA (£6.00) was the drummer's share, which I could not verify as money exchanges are never public and all agreements are verbal. This private exchange of money contrasts with the very public display of donations to *griots* during public performances by audience members and patrons.

3. This denial has to do with the traditionally negative connotations that the 'caste' of *géwël* has.

4. Video recording Sabar-events is very common, and so hiring a cameraman and a generator to provide sufficient light for the recording is part of organizing a Sabar-event.

5. *Créations*, from the French verb *créer* (to create), is used locally to refer to new movements and 'choreographies' that are introduced through popular Mbalax videos.

6. Heath (1994) argues against Irvine (1974: 301–3) who claimed that *géwël* in rural areas are less restrained and dance in more provocative styles. Instead Heath argues that from her observations in Kaolack, factors such as education and religion also promoted a more

restrained behaviour, even amongst the *géwël*. In contrast, when no men were present, women from all backgrounds danced in unrestrained ways. My own observations from Dakar are consistent with Heath's – that women from all backgrounds dance in less restrained ways in exclusively female events.

7. Even though Sabar-events are recorded by a cameraman, he is hired by the event's organizers and so the sole copy remains in their possession. As such, the dancing does not find an indiscriminate audience the way music videos do.

8. Even though this is the proclaimed sequence of rhythms of the Sabar repertoire, in reality the sequence of the rhythms is negotiated with the participants, either explicitly when a dancer requests a specific rhythm, or implicitly when the drummers 'eye' their audience and chose to play appropriate rhythms for them specifically, as for example by choosing to play *ceebujen* for younger women and *yabba* for older women.

Chapter 5

The Kinaesthetic of Sabar

Like other dance forms, learning to dance Sabar is not only about replicating movement. It involves the appropriation of a specific aesthetic quality, a specific texture in one's movement that I call here the 'kinaesthetic of Sabar'. This discussion revolves around a distinction between the technique of movement and the *kinaesthetic* of movement. I employ kinaesthetic in a parallel way to Downey who used it in reference to participants' statements of an 'overall quality of movement' that defines Capoeira (Downey 2005: 118).[1] The kinaesthetic of Sabar does not homogenize everyone's dancing. Participants talk about individual and collective *styles* that affect one's movement and are related to one's age, gender, environment and build. Downey makes a similar point in relation to Capoeira practitioners for whom one's 'teacher, personality, social class, race, and even place of origin allegedly inflect his or her kinesthetic' (ibid.: 122). The kinaesthetic of Sabar relates to notions used by practitioners, as I illustrate further in the chapter. I have refrained from using participants' terms, however, to avoid collapsing categories that are at times homonyms, and instead I maintain 'kinaesthetic' as an analytical term. Although an ephemeral notion, the kinaesthetic of Sabar will be given substance through my discussion of pedagogical techniques.

In this chapter I approach the pedagogical techniques used in New York as attempts to overcome certain common problems that students face in approaching the kinaesthetic of Sabar. I argue that these problems are linked to an over-emphasis on movement that permeates the lay Euro-American understanding of dance and informs the context of New York dance classes, and I draw attention to other aspects that are important to participants, namely the role of kinaesthesia as a learning technique.

A Taste of Sabar

To give a sense of some of the aesthetics involved in dancing Sabar in Dakar I will describe one of my first lessons:

Lëmbël Lesson in Dakar, Edited Field Notes, 19 January 2007
Ashtou shows me a short choreography of *Lëmbël* while singing:
    Dagin ginta
    Dagin ginta . . .
    Tas bah, rakin tsakin tsakin kintas!
Ashtou concludes her dancing but continues to sing the rhythmic phrase so that I can imitate what she did. She watches me and comments. I am told to hold my shirt up and to expose my belly. I am shown how to fold up the bottom half of my shirt and hold it up by placing my left elbow against my torso. My palm has to face up, 'as if I'm holding a gourd'. Ashtou places her Motorola RAZRV3 on my palm, I pretend it's a gourd and I practise.

I have to move my bum more. Her hips seem to shake independently from her legs. It looks fluent and effortless. But I can't do it. I can't move my legs and bum at the same time. There is no distinction between the two, she replies, they should be moving together: 'Why can't you move your bum? Make your bum move! *Comme ça!* She shows me again. She is not happy. She places her arms on my hips and shakes them herself. I realize I need to make the movement larger. Her sister-in-law jumps in 'Let her, let her do it'. I try. Ashtou is happy, '*Wa, c'est ca!* [Yes, that's it!]'

I then realized that while imitating Ashtou I had been focusing on how different parts of my body should relate. I was expressing a cultural bias of what is involved in learning to dance, grounded in a lay Euro-American conception of dance. It was not the exact coordination of my legs and hips that Ashtou was interested in but the magnitude of my hip movement. At least that's where I should begin. My face was also important. Ashtou held her head high, her eyes looking up, and carried a wide smile while dancing. She expected me to do the same.

Facial expressions are very important in Sabar. They are so important that when Ashtou's cousins would film us dancing, they would focus on our faces and torsos, ignoring the lower part of our bodies. Smiling is a sign of enjoying oneself and is an indispensable aspect of a Sabar performance. The eyes are also important. Typically one's sight is fixed on a point in the sky, especially when dancing in public events.[2] Other than this, one may also use a 'flirty' look while dancing, often combined with 'mischievous' smiling for a playful performance when dancing amongst friends. A moderated version of this is employed if a dancer's romantic interest is in the audience. Finally, dancing Sabar also involves the proper handling of one's clothes, whether that is moving one's skirt to expose one's legs and *becho* (undergarment), or holding one's shirt up to expose one's belly. Thus dancing Sabar in Dakar includes the right facial expressions and the appropriate handling of one's clothing, as well as choices as to what to dance.

Abdoulaye's NY Sabar Class, Edited Field Notes, 12 July 2006

Abdoulaye walks in the studio ten minutes late, in green silk trousers, a white T-shirt and a shiny diamond earring. Like many teachers, Abdoulaye has a unique teaching style and a 'following' of students. He connects his iPod to the speakers and the room fills with Mbalax. We warm up and stretch for a few minutes. He announces the dance of the day, *kaolack*. He dances a short choreography and goes on to teach us the different steps that compose it. He shows the moves as if he is dancing, with the same relaxed, nonchalant attitude that characterizes Mbalax. He relies primarily on imitation and repetition, and while his style is good at communicating the general 'attitude' one should have while dancing, it does not help those new to Sabar. Newcomers struggle with Abdoulaye because, unlike other teachers, he does not isolate movements, or break them down. It is not only the sequence and the movements but every single aspect of them that seems alien to a novice: the position of the arms, the legs, the waist, the wrists . . . and of course the rhythm . . . As a novice myself, I cannot see what the different parts of the movements are and so I am unable to reproduce them. I am later told that Abdoulaye is not suggested for beginners and I am referred to André who is good at 'breaking down moves'.

The rhythm proves another problem. It is time to 'go across the floor'. We form lines: three students in a line, one line behind another. When going across in lines, the instructor shows a move and each line repeats it while advancing to the opposite side of the room accompanied by the drumming. The drummers start playing and we try to dance. We start 'moving across the floor' but most of us have trouble starting on the right beat. Maybe it's the emphasis on 1 and 3 of western music that confuses me. It seems that as the drummers play, they change from marking the steps of our feet to marking the beats in between; it's as if we are dancing on the soft and not the dominant rhythms. Sometimes we are offbeat. The drummers stare at our legs and hips as if trying to foresee what we'll do. They mark our steps, but I am unable to hear a rhythm in the drumming. None of us get it right. Abdoulaye complains. He tries to help. He claps the rhythm we should be dancing to and asks us to do the same. We do. Then we start dancing. We don't get it. He decides to dance in front of us. We manage to keep up as long as Abdoulaye is there.

My awe and confusion of that day, first of understanding what the movements are, then trying to hear the rhythm and finally trying to put the two together, was shared by many other students in the class. It is common to anyone new to Sabar, and teachers are well aware of it. The different ways in which teachers and students attempt to deal with this provides the grounds for this discussion.

The Morality of Movement

For some students, a restrictive factor to learning Sabar is the moral quality that a movement induces when performed. Some students overcome this with repetition, while others never do and simply refrain from dancing certain dance-rhythms. This 'restriction' is because movements resonate in the world the student inhabits, albeit with different significance. This was the case for Claire, who I considered to be one of the best Sabar students in New York. Claire was not interested in learning the dance-rhythm *lëmbël*, a playful, sensual dance said to be reserved for one's husband and one's bedroom, and only found in exclusively female gatherings in Dakar.[3] Many Sabar students are aware of these connotations and choose to dance *lëmbël* from the safe standpoint of a playful performance. However, Claire did not avoid the dance because of the sexual connotations *lëmbël* holds for the Senegalese but because *lëmbël* movements also resonated with Claire's world. *Lëmbël* emphasizes one's abilities to move one's hips suggestively and the feelings evoked by the movements were strong enough to keep Claire away from the dance. Another Sabar student, Stella, explained that her first obstacle in Sabar was that certain movements made her feel ungraceful – or in her words, 'like an idiot'. Stella's inhibitions were not linked to the movements themselves resonating as such in her world. In fact she found the movements very impressive when performed by the teacher, which is why she wanted to learn them in the first place. It was that these movements felt alien to her habitual way of moving. Only when she attempted to ignore those feelings, she said, was she able to start learning.

Jackson's account of the Kuranko of Sierra Leone highlights the moral aspect of movement which can 'make sense without being intentional in the linguistic sense, as communicating, codifying, symbolising, signifying thoughts or things that lie outside or anterior to speech' (Jackson 1983: 329). It is precisely 'because bodily praxis in initiation imparts knowledge directly . . . [that] the Kuranko do not need to formulate the meaning of the rite in terms of verbal elaborations or moral concepts' (ibid.: 337). Movement, he argued, is 'meaningful' because of its ability to induce a certain feeling in the performer, not because of its communicative power to someone else. Geurts' analysis of the Anlo-Ewe people of Western Africa provides an intriguing account of the links between 'kinaesthetic sensations' (feeling one's body move) and 'dispositional feelings' (Geurts 2002: 75). For the Anlo-Ewe, there is a 'clear connection, or association, between bodily sensations and who you are or who you become' (ibid.: 76). For this reason Anlo-Ewe parents encourage or discourage their children from moving in certain ways. She uses the example of *lugulugu* which, referring to a person's movement as 'swaying, tarrying, dawdling, or moving as if drunk' (ibid.: 75), is also used to denote one's character and behaviour:

> If you move in a *lugulugu* fashion you experience sensations of *lugulugu*-ness and begin thinking in a *lugulugu* way and become a *lugulugu* person, which is then evident to others from the way your *lugulugu* character is embodied in your *lugulugu* walk. Or, if you consistently think in a *lugulugu* way, you would also move in a *lugulugu* fashion and basically develop into a *lugulugu* person. (Geurts 2002: 76)

Movement's ability to evoke feelings becomes more articulate and even accentuated when there are shifts or breaks with one's habitual way of moving (Jackson 1983). As phenomenologist Drew Leder argues, 'the problematic nature of these novel gestures tends to provoke explicit body awareness' (Leder 1990: 30). Such feelings of 'difference', according to anthropologist Sally Ann Ness, are a routine confrontation for dancers when called to perform new movements:

> A dancer, when cast in a given work of choreography, often finds her- or himself facing the challenge of playing a part that may feel completely foreign . . . The style of action to which the performer must conform may seem not only unfamiliar, but distasteful, repugnant, absurd, or dangerous. Yet, his or her obligation, and the challenge . . . is to overcome the initial shocks of an alien style of action and to adapt to it, to fully *assume* it. (Ness 1992: 11)

In New York Sabar classes, some students are able to overcome the initial confrontation with a radically different movement and appropriate it gradually into their habitus, while others choose not to. Stella pushed herself to overcome feeling 'ugly', while Claire for example did not wish to learn *lëmbël*, at least not in the New York setting of male teachers and drummers:

> I don't want to say inappropriate, but that . . . I can't learn if I feel inhibited, or if I feel too self-conscious, I can't learn. I won't really try because I don't wanna look stupid, or I don't wanna do it wrong. And I feel that way about *lëmbël* and I'm just too self-conscious, and I'm not comfortable enough. (Claire, New York, 2008)

The moral quality of movement demonstrates that learning and becoming skilful is not merely 'a shift from being uncomfortable . . . to being at ease' (Harris

2005: 207), or 'to progress from nausea to well being, to feel at home in one's body and the company of others' (Pálsson 1994: 920). Movement is also moral, and in certain instances the induced feelings do not allow this shift to take place, as the case of Claire illustrates. The morality of movement however is only one problem in a longer process of learning Sabar.

Restricted Perception

In *Art and Agency*, Gell attempts to account for our inability to reproduce the image of the object in front of us when we attempt to draw it. When one looks at an object, he explains, one first creates an image of the object in one's mind. She then attempts to draw this image on a page, but a difficulty arises: 'Because one's hand is not actually directly controlled by the visualized or anticipated line that one wants to draw, but by some mysterious muscular alchemy which is utterly opaque to introspection, the line which appears on the paper is always something of a surprise' (Gell 1998: 45). For Gell, one's inability to reproduce realistic copies of an original is essentially due to a muscular problem: the inability of one's arm to reproduce the line of the visual image in one's mind. In life drawing classes, however, instruction is not geared so much towards improving dexterity in handling a pencil – even though they encourage not holding a pencil as when writing so as to explore other possibilities – as changing one's way of viewing the object. In drawing a human face, for example, instructors will often point out our habitual way of seeing faces. They draw attention to what we usually ignore in our day-to-day interactions with others and point out what we tend to (over)emphasize. A novice's drawing will reflect these tendencies and so the forehead and cheeks will take less space on the page. These are the 'blank' spaces in our interactions with others. In contrast, the eyes and the mouth, which typically draw our attention, are given more space. Instructors thus focus students' attention on 'un-seeing' what we habitually see in a human face in order to produce a drawing that is closer to the actual proportions of the face.

The same principle applies to human movement. Our habitus also guides what we see in moving bodies, and to address this, instruction aims at shifting our habitual way of looking. Downey makes a similar observation in learning Capoeira: 'sensing is not just passive reception, but an active seeking out of important stimuli . . . many skills require that a person learns how to look in order to perceive relevant information' (Downey 2005: 34). What we perceive, and what we need to perceive in order to carry out a task, is formulated by Ingold as 'the gradual attunement of movement and perception' (Ingold 2000: 357) in relation to the ever-shifting conditions of the environment. Ingold builds on Gibson's ecological psychology according to which 'learning is an education of attention' (Gibson 1979: 254), a position that resonates well with the learning/teaching techniques in both life drawing and Sabar classes.

This problem of perception is accentuated when reproducing movement by the fact that in contrast to drawing, or other practices that produce a physical record of a process, we do not normally have a record of our dancing to reflect on later, by comparing it with the original. Even when we do, we may still not be able to realize how much our product deviates from the original as we will continue to restrict our 'seeing' by paying attention only to what we consider to be important, and ignoring what we do not. In Sabar, instruction from teachers and feedback from the mirror and other dancers in the class can guide one to identify what it is one is doing wrong:

> and I could see in the mirror that something is off . . . and I might not know, it might take me a couple of classes to figure it out, but finally I would figure it out. I was like 'you know what, my foot has to come out flat, and that's a certain way that it comes out from my knee' . . . So mirrors have been invaluable, I can't even begin to explain! (Claire, New York, 2008)

Anthropologists and sociologists have also used feedback from mirrors, instructors or even physical pain to help to understand what they are called upon to reproduce (Kaeppler 1972, Wacquant 2004, Downey 2005). Feedback, however, is not itself unproblematic. The dancer and the teachers may recognize that something is not right, but may still not know exactly what is wrong. In this case it is not only the students' but also the teachers' perception that stands in the way.

The opaqueness of bodily techniques, especially to those teaching them, has been highlighted by Bourdieu: 'There are heaps of things that we understand only with our bodies outside conscious awareness, without being able to put our understanding into words' (Bourdieu 1990: 166). While this is true, awareness of one's bodily techniques is not a static state, a position that underlines any methodological attempt to employ apprenticeship as a research method. As I illustrate below, the ability to reflect on one's practice fluctuates for both students and teachers alike. Teachers become more aware of what they are doing and devise ways to communicate it, while students learn to identify problems that restrict their learning.

'Breaking It Down'

Teachers in New York use standardized methods, and André was considered the best teacher for beginners as he 'broke down moves'. For example André would explain the 'core step' of Sabar by breaking it down into three jumps:[4]

> Jump number one: step left foot and 'slap' right foot on the floor with a slight turn of the knee to the right.[5]

Jump number two: jump and step right foot first and then left.
Jump number three: it's more like a step but we'll call it jump number three so that they'll go together. Step right foot and then touch with both feet at the same time.

We repeat the sequence a few times and proceed to add the arms. We practise a few times, combining the arms and the legs.

Now let's put it together! five, six, seven . . . jump number one, jump number two, jump number three! That's it! Now you have it! That's all we do, when you see us and you think 'Wow!', that's all we are doing!
(Edited Field Notes, New York, 2006)

'Breaking down moves' is the most common pedagogical technique in New York classes, and students use it as a marker of a good teacher. It is also a technique that teachers develop gradually as they learn it from the established teachers in New York.[6] They recognize its significance as they become increasingly familiar with students' problems. Otherwise, most of the newly arrived teachers rely primarily on imitation, the way they learned and the way they would teach in their home countries. One student told me that André's teaching evolved over the many years he spent teaching in New York.

When 'breaking down moves', students' attention is directed on specific parts of the body. Some teachers use counts to teach movements, thus fixing each part of the movement to one, two, three, four . . . etc. This technique makes movements 'visible' and also helps students to remember the sequence of movements. 'Breaking down a move' may be good at communicating the technical aspect of the movement (i.e. the body's position in space), but it does not transmit the aesthetic quality of the movement. Fixing movement to time can help one to remember the duration of a movement and the sequence of different parts of the movement, but it also carries the danger of distorting the movement. In fact, it takes one's attention away from the overall aesthetic, resulting in a mechanical movement characterized by artificial rhythmic stops. In the following section I explore how teachers attempt to address this problem.

Restricted Action

Another problem to learning is our *hexis*, our habitual way of moving. Perhaps the most illustrative example of this is the problem that dancers from classical and modern dance training had in learning Sabar. One would have expected trained dancers to have an advantage in learning Sabar because of their extensive training in remembering and reproducing movement. Interestingly however, many of them had common problems. The following description was provided by a student in the class, herself a former dancer of classical and modern dance:

> I see a lot of dancers like roooolling . . . Rooolling . . . And I would see myself . . . or my other thing was from ballet . . . pointing! And pointing! Pointing! . . . I needed mirrors to break me of my other dancing habits. (Claire, New York, 2008)

Claire's distinction between rolling and pointing highlights how in the classical dance tradition the hands and the feet often 'lead' the movement. In contrast, the movement in Sabar appears to originate in the joints, the knees and the elbows. The hands and feet seem to move only as a result of that initial movement in the joints. This articulation is important enough to make a movement look or not look like Sabar.

In contrast to dancers with a classical training, students familiar with West African-related dance forms seemed to be better at performing Sabar. An illustrative example comes from a university Djembé dance class where the teacher would hold auditions at the beginning of each semester. Students had to be able to imitate the teacher's Djembé movements in order to qualify for the class. Dancers with training in ballet and modern dance were often rejected because of their body posture and inability to flex their feet, lower their body and contract their chest and pelvis. In contrast, students were often more successful if they had had no previous dance training or if they came from dance traditions that share common aesthetics with West African dances, such as Diaspora dances like Haitian and Afro-Caribbean, or popular U.S. forms like hip hop. These students excelled due to their ability to imitate not only the movements, but also a certain aesthetic quality that ought to characterize their dancing.

In one of Bourdieu's ethnographic accounts of *hexis*, he analyses how the bodily techniques of the peasant in rural France, 'the heaviness of the gait, the poor cut of the clothes, and the clumsiness of the expression' (Bourdieu 2004: 583), are identified by urbanites as definitive of the peasant and translated into an economic and social standing. When outsiders' perception is internalized by the peasant, Bourdieu argues, it leads to a decrease in the peasant's chances of getting married. Bourdieu qualifies that this depends on the degree of the peasant's self-awareness. In a parallel way, in New York City classes, one's habitus and closeness to the kinaesthetic of Sabar is treated as cultural capital through which some students acquire prestige over others, based on their dancing abilities. However, to what extent a student finds it easy or difficult to incorporate new Sabar movements also depends on the individual's reflexivity. For example, even though Claire came from classical dance training, she was one of the best dancers by the time I met her. This was partly due to her being very critical and reflexive of her dancing. She compared her movements to others' to identify those linked to her classical training, and actively sought feedback from the advanced dancers and teachers in the class. Thus even though one's habitus affects one's ability to learn, one's reflexivity is also important.

The process of embodying skills has been analysed from a phenomenological standpoint by Leder. As a skill becomes more habitual it falls to the background of our awareness. In turn, new skills we are called to incorporate bring our awareness to the forefront, only to recede again when the new skill has been 'incorporated'. Taken 'from the latin *corpus*, or "body", the etymology of this word literally means to "bring within a body"' (Leder 1990: 31). What Leder calls 'incorporation' turns a once novel skill into the body's 'own corporeal history' (ibid.: 32), the next departing point from which the body will be called to learn something new:

> I act from not just my present organs, but a bodily past that tacitly structures my responses . . . it is also via incorporation that abilities sediment into fixed habits . . . Over time they simply disappear from view. They are enveloped within the structure of the taken-for-granted body from which I in*habit* the world. (Leder 1990: 32)

In this way, 'the lived body constantly transforms its sensorimotor repertoire by acquiring novel skills and habits' (Leder 1990: 30). To emphasize this notion of 'incorporation', Ingold argues that 'skills, then, far from being added on to a performed body, actually grow with it. In that regard they are fully part and parcel of the human organism, of its neurology, musculature, even anatomy, and so are as much biological as cultural' (Ingold 2000: 360). Thus, the dancer called to learn Sabar is a dancer already habituated in other ways of moving, and so, in learning, the dancer has to depart from her habituated sense. In the following I will explore the teaching techniques used to challenge students' habitual ways of moving. As will be shown, the techniques complement each other in aiming first at the technical competence of movements and then gradually at a specific aesthetic quality.

Movement as 'Natural'

> 'My Aha! moment' happened . . . I was doing the simple walk in *Sounou* [Djembé dance-rhythm]: walk-walk-walk-together, walk-walk-walk-together, but I was doing this: [imitates walking in a ballet posture], and 'Wait a minute! I don't walk that way! They're just walking and stopping and going like this'. That was 'my Aha! moment', when I stopped thinking about the fact that I had to do it right and I finally listened to the teacher say to me 'it's natural to put your left foot forward and your right arm forward, that's how you balance yourself. Just walk Vicky!' (Djembé teacher, New York, 2006)

Djembé and Sabar movements are often discussed as 'natural' to the body. Other than a descriptive term that aims at a specific aesthetic quality, 'natural' is seen as the essential characteristic of West African dances, and teachers would rationalize this in different ways. André for example would say that Sabar is natural to the body and would link movements to human anatomy. He explained that if we know how our bodies work we will perform the movements as they are supposed to be, while avoiding physical pain and exhaustion. It is 'natural' to lift our leg and not worry where it lands. That way we will not get tired. If we try too much, if we lift our leg too high, we will get tired or get pain.

Lisa employed a similar, more elaborate technique in teaching Djembé. In contrast to dance traditions that 'force' bodies into certain positions, Lisa would argue that West African dance is built from, and on, natural movements.

> The difference between ballet and African is that ballet is restricted; movement is restricted. [In] African there's no restriction, no limits, it knows no boundaries. (Lisa, New York, 2006)

Lisa would draw attention to how the different parts of the body are connected and how this 'connectivity' influences the movement of the rest of the body. She would encourage her class to examine each step before attempting to imitate it: 'Where does the movement begin? What happens next? Don't just do the step! Examine it first!' She would then guide us through the process: 'When the leg goes back, where does the body go?' 'Back' we would answer and continue with the rest of the movement. 'When your arms do this, what does your upper body do?' Lisa would distinguish between moving a body part and that part being moved as an extension of a movement that originated elsewhere:

> It's like when you see someone you notice that the arm is moving, but in actuality there is no moving the arm but rather the arm is moving because the back is going backwards . . . You shouldn't try so hard, since everything is connected, everything is gonna move! (Lisa, New York, 2006)

In this way, Lisa would draw our attention to what she called 'the mechanics' of the body, pointing out that Djembé made full use of these.

The rhetoric of Djembé and Sabar being 'natural' of course contradicted students' initial experience in which movements felt alien, ungraceful and awkward. When teachers demand from the students 'the adoption of new corporeal uses, they call for a veritable change in "nature", since bodily habitus is what is experienced as most "natural", that upon which conscious action has no grip' (Bourdieu 2004: 584). 'Natural' was perhaps the way teachers experienced the movements, not of course due to an inherent quality of the movements but because of their own habituation.

Natural as an Aesthetic

> And now the arms! Relax the arms! Don't worry about getting them right, they have to be relaxed! What's wrong? Do you have a cord in your arm? (André, New York, 2008)

'Natural' was also used to encourage a certain 'aesthetic' in our movement, to encourage fluency. The desired 'relaxed' aesthetic was compromised when movements were 'broken down' to smaller, independent constituents. André would often use metaphors and creative imagery to communicate the attitude of the movement. The leg should fall on the floor like 'fabric, one leg is chasing the other leg, kisses the other leg'. During a 'pause' movement, we were once told to stand back, shift our weight back, bring our left arm in front of us and stare at our wrist, like 'You're looking at your watch ... Take your time, have a good look! You're looking? What time is it? IT'S TIME TO BREAK IT DOWN!!!!' Similar to André, Abdoulaye would encourage us to 'bring it up!', to 'break it down!' or to 'dance with more energy!' when the movements were intended for solos. In contrast he would prompt us to be more relaxed for the movements that function as 'glue' or as introduction to solos. In fact 'relax' was perhaps the verb most commonly used in Sabar classes. It describes a very important aesthetic in Sabar and the most common in Mbalax. At the same time, the verb emphasizes the importance of movement looking fluent and effortless, and not fragmented or mechanical.

Because students in New York seem to face similar problems in achieving a certain aesthetic texture in their dancing, teachers have standardized ways of addressing these. Not all teachers rely on imagery. Others, for example, would simply ask students to observe them and repeat the movements again and again. Repetition, as will be seen further on, is also the predominant way of learning in Dakar and the technique most often used by dancers when teaching other dancers. First, however, I wish to explore a learning technique considered important by many participants that is not part of the teachers' but of the students' repertoire.

Learning through Feeling

> I could *feel* it! And the thing is when I found myself doing things that I wasn't taught, that I would catch reactions from other people, the teacher's reaction, the drummer's reaction... so when I would do something and all of the sudden 'I think there's a head thing and I'm pretty sure I do it right!' – like, 'cos in *farwu jar* there is a head dip, so I just found myself doing it ... I saw it and then I felt it and you know, he never taught it! And I was like 'This is totally in my blood! Like wow, I can't believe, like I could just feel it and do it unconsciously and ... that's when, 'woo hoo!' (Claire, New York, 2008)

Here Claire describes learning as a feeling. She *felt* that she had learned the move, a feeling validated by the feedback she received from dancers and drummers. Many dancers discussed 'feeling' as an important aspect of their learning. Vicky for example explains how she mastered a movement when she stopped focusing on how the movement looked and focused instead on how it looked like it *felt*. This knowledge was triggered by a suggestion from a teacher:

> 'Feel the movement, don't try to mimic what I'm doing, think about how I feel and how my body feels'; and I closed my eyes and I felt the movement and she was like 'that's it!' and then you develop that . . . Because again, you don't know how you look when you are doing something, and a lot of people when they are dancing they concentrate on how they look and not on how the movement feels.

Vicky encourages her students to do the same, to focus on how a movement feels rather than how it looks. When students ask her 'Well then why does it look like this when you do it and like that when I do it?' she replies that her body is different and so the movement cannot but look different. 'My arms are hyper extended, my legs are hyper extended and I have a stretch. Your body does not have those facilities. And I say, with dance, you shouldn't try to look like me. You should try to look like you!' In Vicky's words, the basis for imitating how a movement *feels* is the idea that bodies are different. As a trained ballet dancer, the same movement cannot but look different when performed by Vicky as opposed to one of her students. Accordingly, when imitating how someone else looks, one should not imitate the movement itself but rather the *kinaesthetic* of another person's moving body. For Vicky, one should embrace the difference of bodies and focus not on how the bodies move through space, but rather on how they look like they *feel* when doing so.

Many dancers articulated this emphasis on how a movement looks like it feels, as opposed to how the body looks in space. In Michelle's view, in contrast to ballet, feeling is important in Sabar:

> To me it's about how you *feel* it. Sabar is not like ballet; in ballet there's a certain precision to technique. In Sabar there's technique, but if the emphasis is not on the right place it will look crazy even though in the mirror it might look like you're doing almost the same thing as the other person. But the thing is that if you don't get the emphasis of that feeling . . . its just movement and you can look at yourself in the mirror, 'OK, I'm doing that certain movement' – but if the emphasis is not on the right place it will look wrong.

Michelle here articulates 'feeling' in terms of an emphasis in movement. Earlier, Claire argued for the importance of the mirror in helping her dancing. Michelle, however, argues that the mirror makes it harder to learn Sabar as it emphasizes the body's position in space, over the different emphasis placed on various parts of the body. Her suggestion to students:

> Don't look at yourself. What does it look like? See you gotta be able to look at and see where the emphasis is. Is the emphasis on the movement at the back or the front? Is my weight seating forward or back?' You know, those are the kinds of things you have to get.

For Vicky, Uptown classes facilitate learning by encouraging students to rely on *feeling* the movements. This is because they are mostly held in high school gymnasiums that do not have mirrors:

> When you're taking ballet, you are used to the mirror; in the gym, there's no mirror! It forces you to understand your body and the mechanics of moving and placement, you know. And so, I have to know what a movement is versus looking at it and seeing if I did it right.

Learning through 'feeling' a movement is not unique to Sabar and Djembé. Downey argues that Capoeira instructors 'know well how a movement feels and how to do it without knowing how it looks' (Downey 2005: 43). So, he continues, 'a phenomenological analysis of imitating suggests that the process does not require a visual image of the self' (ibid.). The dual capacity of movement to be experienced by the practitioner and seen by an observer is what allows imitation through *kinaesthetic empathy*: 'while the results of movement can be seen and heard, they are primarily received by the person doing the moving as felt experience, as kinaesthesia' (Sklar 2000: 72). Kinaesthetic empathy highlights the intersubjective nature of learning, whereby imitation is a complex phenomenon that uses multiple sense modalities: 'the reception of dance for the dancer occurs as an ongoing translation between visual and kinaesthetic modalities in a process of "kinaesthetic empathy"' (Sklar 2008: 105). Kinaesthesia refocuses our attention onto the performer and the experiential aspect of dancing, while de-emphasizing the role of the observer and of movement as observed. Kinaesthesia also emphasizes the temporality of movement.

Approaching the Kinaesthetic in Dakar

Having discussed the pedagogical techniques employed in New York, I turn to how the 'kinaesthetic of Sabar' is learned in Senegal. As the next chapter addresses the established local pedagogical techniques in detail, here I will only address the more general framework. Children in Senegal seem to learn the way New York students do, in reverse. As I discussed, New York students first learn the changes of the body's position in space and time, while the kinaesthetic of the movement arrives much later through continuous exposure to dance classes. However, in the case of Senegal, the kinaesthetic of the movement appears first, while the articulation of the movement follows.

Most of the nights with no electricity in Dakar I spent in the kitchen of my hosts, a French expatriate family in an upper-middle-class neighbourhood of Dakar. The kitchen was the domain of Adama, the Senegalese *femme du ménage* (maid). Knowing I was in Senegal for dance, Adama would often call out to her daughter to dance: 'Mame, kaay fecc!' We would clap and Mame Yassine would jump up and down, lifting her right leg slightly, imitating the 'core step' of Sabar. Mame Yassine's dancing was not articulate but was characterized by the kinaesthetic of Sabar. A few months later I realized that this way of learning was not specific to Mame Yassine. In Sabar-events in Dakar, pre-adolescent children rarely jump in the circle to dance. They linger around the edges of the circle, imitating what the older women are dancing in the centre. This way they first acquire the kinaesthetic of Sabar, while the articulation of the movement and how it relates to the rhythm arrive later through gradual exposure to the dance-rhythms.

The kinaesthetic of Sabar is not taught in a systematic way in New York or Dakar. Most of the teachers I trained with did not address the kinaesthetic, even though they would often point at the lack of an aesthetic quality in my movement. Fatou would often tell me, 'You have the move, but it's not beautiful'. She used the term 'feeling'[7] (in English) to denote what I was lacking. When I asked her to explain what she means by that, she used her arm to trace a current through her body, starting from her feet and passing through her head towards the sky. However, she did not provide any suggestions as to how I could improve. Instead, when we concluded our lessons, she told me that knowing some movements means that I now have the 'key', and suggested I accompany drummer Modou to the events he plays so as to expose myself to a lot of dancing. For Fatou, 'feeling' could not be taught but would 'arrive' through my attendance of Sabar-events, in the same way that children learn. This approach is not available to New York students, where Sabar classes are part of a financially conscious setting and their structure is underlined by Euro-American understandings of dance and learning.

This chapter has explored some of the pedagogical techniques used to communicate movement in New York classes. I have discussed common difficulties that students face in learning Sabar and more general problems of learning when one is called to reproduce movements alien to one's *hexis*. Where appropriate, comparisons have been made with teaching techniques in Djembé. I suggested that what the students and teachers ultimately strive for, through different pedagogical techniques, is a specific aesthetic quality of movement that I refer to as the 'kinaesthetic of Sabar'. I have highlighted the importance of learning through feeling for the New York participants, where students approach the kinaesthetic of Sabar through 'kinaesthetic empathy'.

Notes

1. A different definition of 'kinaesthetic' in reference to Sabar is offered by Castaldi: 'the idiom of Sabar dancing defines an ethic of aesthetic presentation and public display in which an erotic femininity is vigorously performed and noisily supported. I call this relationship between ethics, aesthetics and kinetics established through dancing *kinaesthetic*' (Castaldi 2006: 80).

2. Other anthropologists have provided explanations for this but I never received a consistent explanation from informants. Most were surprised at my observation and stated that this is the way it is done, while someone claimed that it probably helps dancers to concentrate. Tang (2007) states that it is to avoid the drummer's sight.

3. An exception to this is the drummers, who are always male. Castaldi argues (2006) that this is due to the wide perception of the *géwël* as having ambivalent sexuality.

4. Different dance-rhythms have different movements but this is generally considered the 'core step' of Sabar.

5. This is for someone right-legged and so it is reversed if the person is left-legged.

6. This is similar to how knowledge is shared by Senegalese in other countries and by migrant networks more generally (Carter 1997: 37).

7. Tang (2007) notes the word 'feeling' (in English) is used by Sabar drummers to denote someone's 'style' of playing.

Chapter 6

Hearing Movements, Seeing Rhythms

It's a balance, nasty balance, and a drummer will say to a dancer 'Really dance, so I can play', and the dancer will say 'Well play, and I'll dance'.
(African American teacher, New York, 2006)

Anyone who has experimented with West African dances is familiar with the 'mystical' connection between the dancing and the drumming. It features prominently in the discourses of the students. Dancing to the rhythm is one of the first problems students face in learning West African dance forms. Here I explore the relationship between dancing and drumming in Sabar, through the pedagogical technique used to communicate rhythm and movement in Sabar, and discuss the aesthetic of improvisation embedded in this technique.

I employ the term 'aesthetic' following dance anthropologist Kaeppler to denote the criteria by which one is evaluated (Kaeppler 2003: 153). So aesthetics here denotes the parameters that qualify someone as a good Sabar dancer by others competent in the form.[1] Throughout the book I have suggested that Sabar dance-rhythms are continuously redefined as they circulate through different dancers and performance settings, and that there is no one authority or authentic setting for Sabar. This entails different Sabar genres having different aesthetics as, for example, ballet dancers are praised for their technique, high jumps and grandiose movements. Yet as I noted, the different genres in Sabar are not distinct spheres of performance but are linked through the dancers and movements that circulate through them (Castaldi 2006). An aesthetic which both lay and professional dancers, including ballet dancers, evoked as an indication of a 'good dancer' of Sabar, is the aesthetic of improvisation. Furthermore, the frame of reference evoked for the assessment of a good dancer is the public Sabar-event.

A good dancer is one who creates new, exciting *créations*, improvised solos with no hesitation. Improvisation however is not taught to foreign students. Instead, foreign students learn prearranged choreographies, primarily by dancers from traditional ballets. There, the movements are arranged in choreographies, and students are expected to reproduce them the same way. These preset choreographies do not equip one to perform in public Sabar-events as improvisation is based on the dancer having a good understanding of how the rhythm relates to the dancing. The starting point for this discussion then is the problem that New York students face in understanding and dancing to Sabar rhythms.

The Problem of Rhythm

I don't remember having a specific problem taking up the dance style. But the rhythm . . . I couldn't hear *baar mbaye*. I used to love *kaolack* and *niarigoron* 'cos I could hear them so clearly. (Michelle, New York, 2008)

Edited Field Notes, New York, 12 July 2006
Sabar drumming, for the uninitiated, sounds like gunfire. There seems to be absolutely no hint of rhythm. How many counts are in a musical meter seems to change from 1-2, 1-2 to 1-2-3-4-5, 1, 1-2 . . . While the rhythmic phrase is repeated, it lasts too long, making it difficult to remember. I decide to memorize the rhythm of Abdoulaye's dancing, and maintain an internal rhythm in my dancing while ignoring the drums. I have completely detached myself from the drumming and it seems to work. I manage to dance to the rhythm, not because I understand it but by ignoring it. The choreography too seems unbalanced. Abdoulaye gives us a combination where we do the step, then wait for a couple of beats and finish with a two-count hip move . . . There is no three, as one would expect and so we're left in limbo; we linger there until the drummers play the phrase from the beginning and we repeat the sequence. Abdoulaye says we can take from three to five rhythms to complete the movement; that it's up to us. I'm not sure the tempo is consistent. It seems to have slowed down. Abdoulaye often tells the drummers what to play. He seems unhappy with their drumming. He takes the drumstick off one drummer and shows him what to play. He often gets up, shows us a move, and then sits down and drums to accompany us.

(Not) Communicating Rhythm

The rhythm remains a persistent problem for New York students. Most teachers rely on repetition, expecting that students' understanding will gradually increase. Some encourage students to clap the rhythm, but this has only short-term effects. Students can dance while clapping but will not necessarily be able to identify when to start if the drumming stops and starts again. Others use the established pedagogical and performing guide of Sabar by using specific syllables to communicate the rhythm. This however requires special knowledge on the part of the students and so is reserved for advanced classes. And so students complain that teachers do not understand their problems:

> There's certain things I know the guys [Senegalese drummers and teachers] take for granted, or the rhythm . . . they were hard for me to learn. Instead of people just saying to me 'Oh, can't you just hear it?' There's steps inside *baar mbaye*; if you ask me to 'do that step' I will get lost every time because I have trouble doing that rhythm, I have trouble to feel it, how the step goes. If I had to teach that to somebody I would teach it knowing what my challenges were. (Michelle, New York, 2008)

Teachers' lack of emphasis on rhythm may be due to their inability to verbalize their skill (Bourdieu 1990: 166). However, the failure to communicate rhythm is not only a problem with the teachers' understanding and their ability to foresee what students have difficulties with, but more generally with the way the classes are standardized and taught in New York City.

New York Sabar classes are primarily about dancing. If one wants to learn the rhythm, one can opt to take drumming classes. In the dance classes students are taught prearranged choreographies of movements for the different dance-rhythms – *baar mbaye, ceebujen, farwu jar*, etc. Choreographies are then repeated at the end of each class. The dancing is set and the drumming follows the choreography. So students can anticipate the next rhythmic phrase and only need to remember the choreography. When students perform individual solos at the end of each class, they tend to perform short parts of choreographies they have learned. The drummers accordingly adjust the drumming to the choreographies, which they recognize from previous classes.

The arrangement of movements into choreographies can be attributed to the dance teacher's trajectory. As discussed (Chapter 4), the majority of them are dancers from traditional ballets where dances are organized into choreographies to be performed on stage. This format has become standardized when teaching foreigners, and students expect it. In fact, students evaluate teachers depending on whether they teach in this format. In addition, Senegalese teachers and New York students understand differently their roles in the class. In Senegal most of my teachers were suggested to me by virtue of being good dancers. The idea of a good teacher was not articulated, or not distinguished from being a good dancer. Along with the idea that someone learns by being enveloped in a certain environment rested the idea that the responsibility for learning lies with the one who learns. In contrast, in New York classes, teachers were held directly responsible for their ability to communicate movement at a level that was comfortable to students. The Senegalese teachers who were preferred by students were those who appropriated the role of the teacher and what this role entailed in a Euro-American understanding.

The standardized way of teaching Sabar is very important considering the economic relationship between teachers and students. Students can choose between teachers depending on how satisfied they are. This has a direct effect on the teachers, as for many teaching dance constitutes their main income. Thus teachers have a strong financial incentive to adjust to the 'standardized' structure of Sabar classes in New York City. Similar to Bourdieu's discussion (2004), the socio-economic setting here affects the relationship between bodily techniques and self-reflection, encouraging the adjustment of teachers' understandings to those of the students.[2] Furthermore, accommodating students' expectations can also be considered to be teachers' cultural capital as *griots*, as *griots* receive financial compensation for catering to their patron or audience. Thus New York classes of Sabar are seen as primarily to do with movement. They thus teach choreographies, while Sabar rhythms are seen merely as an accompaniment to the choreography. This leads to students' persistent problems in understanding the rhythms.

Against Cumulative Knowledge

Students in New York are given a 'stock' of knowledge that they are expected to reproduce: movements arranged in choreographies. Rhythm is not explicitly taught but is learned through exposure to many dance classes. The advanced students gradually acquire an understanding of the rhythm, and so their dancing and the dancing of the teachers act as guidelines for the newcomers to follow during class. With time and exposure comes the refinement of one's technique, a broader repertoire of movements and choreographies, and only later comes the ability to 'hear' the rhythm and coordinate one's dancing with the drumming. As I show, however, rhythm in Sabar is an intrinsic aspect of dancing and not merely a final touch in one's primarily dancing performance.

The way Sabar is taught in New York seems to conform to what Lave calls 'the culture of acculturation' (Lave 1990: 310), which she argues defines schooling and educational institutions (ibid.: 310–11). According to this view, 'knowledge' is the sole property of the individual who accumulates it, to different degrees through exposure to teaching:

> Conventional explanations view learning as a process by which a learner internalizes knowledge, whether 'discovered', 'transmitted' from others, or 'experienced in interaction' with others … It establishes a sharp dichotomy between inside and outside, suggests that knowledge is largely cerebral, and takes the individual as the nonproblematic unit of analysis. (Lave and Wenger 1991: 47)

As knowledge 'enters' and rests with the individual and is available for future retrieval this view treats the 'person in terms of a container' (Pálsson 1994: 903) (for critiques of this view, see Lave and Wenger 1991, Ingold 2000). Alternative conceptions of learning that locate learning 'in the processes of co-participation, not in the heads of individuals' (Hanks 1991: 13) offer a better way to conceptualize the established pedagogical and performing technique used for improvisation in Sabar. Lave and Wenger argue that learning is located in the co-participation of the apprentice and a 'community of knowledge and practice' (Lave and Wenger 1991: 29). Similarly, Ingold emphasizes the importance of the environment in the learning and carrying out of a skill, arguing against theories that want knowledge or a skill to be the property of the individual, conceptions which draw a line between the person and the environment and ignore the unique circumstances in which a task is always carried out (Ingold 2000). Novices learn by being guided on how to engage and attend to the environment with the purpose of carrying out an intention. Learning is the 'continual adjustment or "tuning" of movement in response to an ongoing perceptual monitoring of the emergent task' (ibid.: 353). Thus skills 'are developed through an active exploration of the possibilities afforded by the environment, in the choice of materials and structural supports, and of bodily capacities of movement, posture and prehension' (ibid.: 359). In the following section I explore how these ideas contribute to a better understanding of movement and rhythm in Sabar.

Guided Improvisation

During my first lessons in Senegal, Fatou would teach me a short sequence of movements and then ask me to dance along to the drumming. As Sabar drumming is polyrhythmic, most foreigners struggle to identify what rhythm to dance to. Even if the movements are expected to follow one another, which was the case with Fatou's preset choreography, they do not necessarily 'fit' to the rhythm. So counting 'one, two, three' does not help. Sometimes a move has to begin before the previous one has ended. Not being familiar with the rhythm, I could not predict when to finish a move. As Fatou was an experienced teacher with foreigners she had ways of dealing with this: 'Finish the move!', 'Don't finish the move!' she would call out. I understood that it was the rhythm and not the movements that should guide me but I still could not hear the rhythm. Fatou then asked me to clap the rhythm played by the drummer. I managed this fine but did not seem to dance to it properly. Instead, she suggested that I sing along with her: 'Rau Taki, Rau Taki . . .' telling me not to rely on the drummers. If I wanted to learn to dance properly, she said, I had to also learn these words. The significance of this was not immediately obvious to me, so I set Fatou's singing aside for a while and relied on another dancer's suggestion to think of Sabar as jazz.

Tony explained that the rhythmic basis may not be articulated in Sabar by any of the instruments but only used to improvise upon. However, even if silent, the rhythmic basis is always there. Based on this it seems that when dancing one should not focus on trying to hear a base rhythm, but rather on trying to maintain the rhythm with one's dancing.[3] This suggests that the dancing and the drumming are somewhat independent from each other. Not entirely so. The dancer may not be dancing to a rhythm played by the drums but the dancer's movements are often articulated by the drumming. For this to happen, the drummer and the dancer need to share a common repertoire of movements or potential combinations of movements. In Sabar, movements and drum strokes are organized in short phrases called *bàkks* and expressed verbally through the use of specific syllables, a common technique throughout West Africa. As Kubik argued early on, 'describing' rhythms 'by means of verbal or purely syllabic formulas' is used for teaching and learning as well as to 'identify associated rhythm forms' (Kubik 1979: 223). Wober pointed out later that 'West African cultures include an elaboration of the proprioceptively and aurally perceived world. Thus, music is an extension of speech, rhythm an extension of movement' (Wober 1991: 33). Patricia Tang's ethnography (2007) looks at these verbal utterances which she calls 'mnemonics' from the perspective of Sabar drummers. Tang provides a detailed account of corresponding syllables to drum strokes, but carefully notes that while specific phonemes correspond to specific drum strokes, the phonemes used may vary from one *géwël* family to another. Castaldi has referred to the same method as 'singing the rhythm' and has recognized some of its value as a pedagogical tool from the perspective of the dancers (Castaldi 2006: 133). These 'sung rhythms' can help a dancer to remember a dancing sequence and argues that the singing 'represents a form of movement analysis that aids dancers in learning and remembering the dance' (ibid.: 136). However, Castaldi does not acknowledge the full potential of this tool, which is not only pedagogical but also a practical guide for improvisation when performing.

In fact the importance of this tool lies not in its rigidity but in its flexibility and the possibilities it provides to those with the knowledge to employ it. The syllables verbalize rhythmic phrases, whether these are of a specific Sabar *rythme* (in French), or *bàkks* and function as both the frame and guidelines for improvisation.[4] In the absence of drums they can be used to communicate a certain *bàkk* or a *rythme* from the Sabar repertoire: *farwu jar, ceebujen, baar mbaye, yabba* or *lëmbël*. As *rythmes* also connote dances, there are different movements specific to each *rythme* even though many *rythmes* share common movements. Below I provide examples of how the introductions to the two rhythms *ceebujen* and *baar mbaye* are verbalized. My drum teacher Modou would sing the introduction to *ceebujen*:

Rau dau rau dau rau dau gin, ran da gin, ran da gin
Rau dau rau dau rau da gin, tata gin, tata gin, tata gin, tata gin, tata gin, tata gin

In contrast, the introduction to *baar mbaye* he sang as:

Basa kin taki, Kin kin kin taki, Basa kin taki, Baar mbaye taki
Basa kin taki, Kin kin kin taki, Taki taki taki taki taki taki taki
Bacha kin kin taki, Basa kin taki, Kin kin kin kin

Each of these syllables denotes the type of drum stroke and the type of movement that can accompany the drum stroke. As mentioned by Tang (2007), these syllables are not specific but interchangeable with others that can be used to denote the same type of drum stroke. The dancers I worked with explained that the use of these syllables is not exclusive to the *géwël*, but also used by non-*géwël* professional dancers and drummers. I did not verify whether their choice of syllables depended on the *géwël* family they may have trained with, but that would not be unlikely. *Rythmes* seem to be taught to younger members of a *géwël* family at an early age. My teacher Ashtou for example would often sing a Mbalax tune or short *bàkks* to her baby niece while rocking her to the rhythm, a practice I noticed amongst many dancers.

Returning to the *rythmes*, Tang explains that from a percussionist's perspective *bàkks* are overlaid in each *rythme*: a '*bàkk* is a strictly musical term, referring to a musical phrase played on the Sabar drums' (Tang 2007: 112). She continues that a *bàkk* is usually longer and more elaborate than a *rythme*, which is a typically shorter musical phrase played repeatedly. Furthermore:

> The *bàkks* are the sites of *géwël* creativity. Some *bàkks* represent verbal text; some are dedicated to particular people or families; others are simply creative compositions or examples of virtuosity. *Bàkks* can be handed down from generation to generation, some unchanged, others modified over time; and every day, new *bàkks* are created, whether by an individual or a Sabar group as a whole. (Tang 2007: 97)

Some *bàkks* are familiar to the audience and played repeatedly in street-Sabars. Typically, lay, female dancers in street-Sabars will rise from their seats, enter the circle and perform a short solo to a *bàkk* while facing the drummers. They will then return to their seats in the audience. Just as *bàkks* are sites of creativity for drummers, they are also sites of creativity for dancers. Lay dancers will mostly dance to recognizable *bàkks*, but *géwël* and professional dancers will take more liberty in monopolizing the dance floor, often creating their own *bàkks* by guiding the drummers to follow their movements. A *bàkk* can be danced in different ways, *ça depend à toi*. However, improvisation is guided, as the choice of movements depends on the drum strokes of each *bàkk*. For example, in dancing *baar mbaye say say*, the *bàkk* is sung:

Baar mbaye Say Say
Kin kin kin Taki
Baar mbaye Say Say
Kin kin kin Taki
Baar mbaye Say Say
Kin kin kin Taki
Raou tararararararararaou kin Taki
Raou tararararararararaou kin Taki
Tarapai tat ta ta [a pause for the dancer]
Kin taki
Tsang tsang tsang

The different drum strokes suggest possibilities for appropriate movements. Movements can be substituted with others of the same nature. For example *Tourourourou* can be used to denote the core Sabar step, while it can also signify a turn for the dancer. Similarly, *Taki* is used to denote a sudden end of a phrase, or a sudden stop within a phrase, and as such should be accompanied by an abrupt/ sudden movement. Whether that is a sudden movement of the pelvis forward or a slight push of the hips to one side, the choice lies with the dancer. For example Fatou showed me to push my pelvis forward while placing my right arm on my lower back, while her sister chose to also mark the rhythm by 'beating' the side of her right fist on the side of her hip. These are only two variations and it is important for the dancer to know the 'family' of movements – that is, the movements that are understood to be similar, thought to have the same effect and thus be interchangeable.

In conclusion, the rhythmic structure of the *bàkk* provides a basis upon which dancers can improvise. Rather than being a mere pedagogical tool to remind the dancer of a preset sequence of movements, *bàkks* and their verbalization guide the dancer in choosing movements. There are many possible movements to accompany a certain drum stroke and it lies within the knowledge, ability and creativity of the dancer to choose one over another. This technique is followed primarily by lay dancers, as more advanced dancers, *géwël* and professional dancers may not remain as 'faithful' to the *bàkks* and may instead take the freedom to monopolize the dance floor with longer solos, guiding the drummers to create their own, unique *bàkks*.

Creative Imitation: Television, the Mirror and the Others

So how does one build the knowledge of a family of movements that allows one to improvise to *bàkks*? When I showed Ashtou's choreographies to her female cousins, instead of getting feedback on my dancing I was shown variations on what I had done. At first, I interpreted this as evidence of my poor performance, which I assumed led them to show me easier moves. My frustration at being given new movements subsided when I realized that they were providing me with a repertoire of *bàkks* and movements I could use interchangeably. The objective was for me to build the knowledge that would allow me to combine movements creatively. This gradual building of a repertoire happens through what I previously discussed as 'creative imitation', which takes place in a variety of settings, from private events in houses, to public dance-events, and finally at a broader level through Mbalax clips broadcast on television (see Chapter 4). Thus in Ashtou's room we would start by imitating the movements in the videos until someone introduced a slight variation. The rest of us would imitate this until someone else introduced a new movement. During this, women would peak glances at their image in the mirror, checking on their dancing and facial composure. Thus learning was not simply imitating but rather a constant back and forth exchange between the dancers. The television Mbalax clips, the mirror and the Others were used to compare and enrich one's movement. This process of 'creative imitation' is also observed in street-Sabars, where the children and adults standing around the circle will often imitate the dancing of the soloist in the centre. To show their appreciation for the soloist's dancing and ability, they might occasionally join the soloist in the centre.

Beyond the private setting of one's home and the public occasions of street-Sabars, creative imitation also works at a national and international level. It underlines the way new movements and choreographies, *créations*, are created and enter the popular dance domain, the clubs and street-Sabars through Mbalax videos on television, or recorded DVDs sold in New York City, only to be improvised upon further and returned to future Mbalax videos. Thus learning to dance Sabar involves not only the imitation of movements but also the knowledge of possible substitutes. One learns by building a 'repertoire' of movements and *bàkks* in the overlapping spheres of one's home, the public Sabar event and the broader national and international spheres given existence through the media. The way movements circulate through these spheres conforms to a very important 'aesthetic' of Sabar, that of improvisation.

Concluding Remarks

A closer look at the pedagogical techniques used to communicate rhythm and movement in Sabar highlights the importance of the aesthetic of improvisation. The technique is also a performing tool that guides the dancers who have the knowledge to use it appropriately as a set of prescribed techniques. However, when Sabar is taught in New York it becomes redefined; it is taught primarily as movement and is divorced from the drumming. This has to do with two assumptions underlying the pedagogical techniques used in New York City regarding dance and the nature of learning. New York classes over-emphasize, de-contextualize and isolate movement, treating it independently from rhythm. The classes are also underlined by assumptions on the nature of learning that view knowledge as something to be accumulated and to rest with the individual. However, to improvise in Sabar one needs to understand the dialectical relationship of movement and rhythm. Building on Lave and Wenger (1991) and Ingold (2000), I argued for the need to understand Sabar as a processual and environed activity. The pedagogical technique and performing guide used in Sabar requires a conception of dancing, as in the act of moving in time and space, to be a relational practice, constantly negotiated with the specific parameters of the performance occasion. This further leads one to question the notion of learning and performing as being distinct. The pedagogical technique and performing guide used in Sabar is best conceived as a process that does not distinguish learning from performance but rather conceives it as shifts in degrees of participation (Lave and Wenger 1991). Here I have focused on one element of the 'environment' of a performance, the rhythm. However, as Heath (1994) has argued earlier, choosing what to dance in Sabar includes a consideration of the demographic of the audience and the occasion of the event, as well as the age, 'caste' and social status of the dancer.

Notes

1. For studies that look at the aesthetics of dance forms from an anthropological perspective, see Kaeppler (1971) and Grau (2003). On the aesthetics of West African dance forms, Thompson has developed the 'aesthetic of the cool' (Thompson 1966), and Dixon-Gottschild discusses the 'geography of the black dancing body' or Africanist aesthetics in body posture and movement (Dixon-Gottschild 2003: 106).
2. Bourdieu discusses the relationship between the techniques of the body and the external appearance between female and male peasants in south-western France. He argues that women's motivation to emulate a 'city' appearance is stronger than the men's, as they see the future benefit of a better marriage. At the same time, attending to their bodies has been a lifelong encouragement by the 'whole cultural system', a behaviour that is by contrast discouraged in boys and men (Bourdieu 2004: 589–90).
3. This observation was also made by Chernoff (1979) in relation to Ghanaian drumming and dancing, and by Browning (1995) for Brazilian Samba.
4. *Rythme*, in French, is used locally to denote the different dance-rhythms of Sabar, such as *baar mbaye* and *ceebujen*. Here I maintain the term *rythme*, in its local use, to refer to these specific dance-rhythms, and to distinguish them from 'rhythm', in English, used analytically.

Conclusion

Moving with Sabar

This study's methodological movement between New York and Dakar had the following aims: firstly, to ground locally theoretical discussions that aim to conceptualize social life and the movement of people and cultural forms in an increasingly interconnected world; and secondly, to explore comparatively pedagogical techniques, ideas of learning, local aesthetics and notions of dance. As a result, this study also addressed how pedagogical techniques are linked to the socio-economic and historical relations of participants.

By means of an ethnographic treatment of the role of the imagination and its relation to social life I argued that the imagination plays an important role in mobilizing U.S. students to West Africa, and West African artists to the United States. A romantic image of Africa lures U.S. students to travel to West Africa while, for the West African artists, Sabar is romanticized as an avenue to a cosmopolitan life. However, I also argued against the way relationships in tourist destinations have been theorized in the literature as 'sex tourism' or naïve love (Hall and Ryan 2001, Oppermann 1999, Seabrook 1996, Truong 1990, Ebron 2002, Castaldi 2006). Through personal narratives and individual trajectories, I showed that the participants' understandings and motivations are varied and layered, and cannot be reduced to approaches that homogenize them. Instead, I have emphasized individual agency, as different participants negotiate unique personal desires that are nevertheless grounded within broader socio-cultural fields of meaning. Romance may lure certain participants, but for others romance is employed strategically in the way Africa is represented, or the way relationships are pursued, in a process that illuminates complex power relations between North American students and West African artists.

I also discussed the continuing relevance of centre–periphery relations (Hannerz 1997) that remain pertinent and 'punctuate' boundaries in the transnational flow of people and cultural forms. The participants' movement, and the availability of the dances in New York, are confronted by the political geography of the different countries they move through. Thus, as Guinea remains politically and economically more unstable than Senegal, Senegal continues to function as a 'bridge' for artists and dance forms to the United States. Individuals navigate these boundaries creatively, negotiating their mobility not only with the government of the host country, but also in the intimate arena of romantic relationships. Thus imagination is always localized and implicates participants in complex power relations. Adding a historical dimension to the role of the imagination and the global flow of cultural forms (Appadurai 1991), I discussed how patterns set in motion in the past form avenues towards similar pursuits in the present, albeit redefined and adapted to a contemporary setting. Thus, West African dances continue to be approached as avenues to cosmopolitan mobility, no longer with the support of the government, but through the pursuit of strategies on the personal level.

Further, through an exploration of the contextualizing moves informants make to acquire a 'context' for the practice of the dance forms, I illustrated that anthropological notions of 'cultural relativity', the 'context' and 'experience of the everyday' in the lives of Others, have transcended the academy and become part of participants' discourses and practices. U.S. students engage in travels to West Africa to acquire a 'context' for their practice. However, while broader discourses may be echoed in participants' contextualizing moves, I have also illustrated individual agency in these moves. This adds another dimension to the study of representations of Africa (Castaldi 2006, Ebron 2002, Mudimbe 1988) that has addressed broad colonial and postcolonial socio-cultural discourses and images, but not how actors interpret these. I have illustrated that while broader discourses are important, individuals have unique ways of conceptualizing their involvement, and so West African dance forms provide the canvas on which participants project personal desires, albeit grounded within broader socio-cultural fields.

Sabar Representation, Politics, Realities

Beyond an avenue to mobility, West African artists approach dance as a form of self-representation, which they can employ to position themselves differently vis-à-vis local audiences, the Dakarois field of dance genres and the international community. They can thus impress local audiences through Mbalax *créations*, present 'tradition' to local and foreign audiences, and position themselves in relation to Western political debates.

I also explored the significance of technology and the shifts it induces in environments of learning and performing Sabar in Dakar. The ability for dance to be recorded and transmitted through television Mbalax clips and the internet allows access to an audience traditionally excluded from the performance of dance, such as older, married, religious women. On the other hand, recorded performances render performances 'static', transcending the temporality of the event and enabling post-event access to an indiscriminate audience, thus challenging traditional performance spaces and expectations. However, while videorecorded performances introduce changes, they also resist them. Thus, the dancing in television Mbalax clips is appropriated by the local aesthetic of improvisation, and so choreographies on television become the grounds for future improvisation by lay and professional Dakarois. Thus, as performance contexts are very important for the kind of Sabar they feature, shifting conditions create tensions of 'appropriateness'.

Sabar also provides the space for the expression of social tensions in New York City. I explored how an analysis of the micro-politics on the dance floor reflects and at times subverts larger political and historical relationships. I argued that while the geographical, socio-economic and intellectual context of the classes predefines, to an extent, the meanings of the class, participants use the dance floor to re-choreograph larger socio-political relationships. I explored the tension between the Uptown and Downtown settings as they draw together participants from different backgrounds with different objectives. These tensions were at times voiced in unique bodily terms through a resistance to the homogeneity that is imposed in a dance class. Participants negotiated space and time to evoke different hierarchical structures and position themselves in relation to others. Two of these hierarchical structures were established by the dancers' approach to the dance forms. Students asserted themselves as good dancers in technique and performance, or 'serious' students by pursuing knowledge of the socio-cultural background of the dance forms. While these two hierarchies could be negotiated by anyone, a third one, established on the grounds of cultural affinity to the forms, could not. In that case, some African American participants, a typically 'mute' group in American history and society, inverted conventional hierarchies in a verbally silent yet bodily assertive manner, silencing Others in the class and defining the event as a 'community' affair. West African teachers and drummers – the 'authorities' of the classes – were often found in the compromising position of having to resist exclusive definitions in order to accommodate a diverse group of students while not alienating community participants. New York classes thus provide the grounds for historical and socio-political relationships between West Africans, African Americans and Other participants to surface and be contested. Dance-events may draw together diverse participants but do not necessarily 'accommodate' multiple meanings. Instead, they provide the grounds for larger issues to be negotiated.

Political relationships are not the only relevant feature of dance, as participants give voice to experiential aspects of the classes. I discussed the notion of 'energy', an important quality of the class experience that is endowed with agency and can thus influence participants in different ways. Energy acquires agency from various aspects of a specific dance-event – the drummers, the dancers, the setting, etc. – and in turn can have a positive or negative effect on the dancing and the drumming. This experiential reality may be hidden from outsiders, as participants explained, and is acquired gradually through increasing participation in dance classes. Such experiential notions emphasize the use of apprenticeship as a methodological tool, as it affords the researcher the status of a full participant, allowing her to cross-reference participants' discourses and claims to reality with participant observation of the events in which this reality is grounded.

Learning and Performing Sabar

This book illustrates that methodologically, by focusing on the pedagogical tools used in other practices, one can unravel the category of dance in different settings 'from the inside'. 'Dance' has traditionally been deconstructed as an analytical term in the anthropology of dance, through comparisons with the 'emic' categories of dance in different ethnographic settings. By exploring what is taught and how pedagogical techniques relate to the different socio-cultural settings of Sabar, this book has provided an ethnographic account of how 'dance' – in this case the phenomenon that is Sabar – is constantly redefined in different settings. Apprenticeship as a research method thus helps to uncover local categories of 'dance' as well as local aesthetics, notions of learning and being.

The Habitus of the Senses

This book has also provided an ethnographic treatment of how the notion of 'habitus' relates to the senses. An important aspect of dance, in the discourses of the participants, is a specific aesthetic quality of one's movement, the 'kinaesthetic of Sabar'. The kinaesthetic is dependent on movement and technique, but also requires different pedagogical approaches than merely learning and replicating a certain movement. Voicing participants' learning methods, I showed how they approach the kinaesthetic through 'kinaesthetic empathy', a technique that emphasizes the experiential aspect of movement. An important restrictive factor to learning Sabar, I showed, is the moral quality of movement. Building on Jackson (1983) and Geurts (2002), I illustrated that movement has the power to communicate 'meaning' to the dancer through kinaesthesia as well as form. In the case of Sabar, some movements resonated negatively with the dancers' own worlds and thus kept them away from learning certain dance-rhythms.

I also showed that the ability to be reflexive and aware of a certain skill is fluctuating and context dependent, not static and impenetrable. At the same time, I argued that the degree of reflexivity of someone is linked to their habitus and socio-economic relationships with others. This was evident in the way dancers with a Euro-American dance training background, although accustomed to attending to their movements, were unable to realize the change in perception that Sabar required of them. On the other hand, Senegalese teachers adapted their pedagogical techniques once in New York in order to communicate more appropriately with American students. This, I suggested, is linked to the economic relationship they hold with their students, as well as to teachers' cultural capital as *griots*, which encourages them to accommodate their students rather than the other way around.

Learning as an Environed Activity

I focused on the problems that New York students face in 'hearing' the rhythms of Sabar and argued that the problem is grounded on two assumptions that underlie New York classes. The first has to do with how 'dance' is conceived in the New York setting, which is conflated with movement while rhythm is considered to be external. The second is related to ideas about learning, namely that knowledge is thought to be internalized and 'accumulated' by the individual, to be available for future retrieval. I argued for the need to conceptualize Sabar as an environed activity, where dancing is always relational to the specific parameters of the environment. My analysis focused on the rhythm, although other aspects are equally important as noted by earlier researchers (Heath 1994). I suggest that such an approach demands an alternative conception of learning than the one employed in New York classes.

Exploring the pedagogical tools employed in Dakar by dancers and drummers, I delineated how the relationship between movement and rhythm is crystallized in the pedagogical and performing guide, and verbalized through specific syllables. This technique also embodies an important aesthetic in Sabar, the aesthetic of improvisation. I concluded, therefore, that a conception of learning along the lines of Ingold (2000) and Lave and Wenger (1991) is more appropriate for learning and performing Sabar. The environment, they argue, is not 'external' to the activity but an intrinsic aspect of it. This conception accounts better for the aesthetic of improvisation, which in fact defines many learning and performing settings of Sabar: learning through 'creative imitation' with friends and Mbalax videos on television or performing in street-Sabars. Further, the above challenge the conception of learning and performing as distinct, as in the case of Sabar it makes sense to conceive it as a shift in degrees of participation in a constellation of activities within a community that shares common understandings about their practice (Lave and Wenger 1991). Contributing to studies on the body and dance, I illustrated how the dancing body in Sabar evinces essentialist discourses of difference. These essentialist differences, however, are ignored when dance moves into the status of a commodity and dancers are faced with a foreign audience, which is what allows male dancers to teach Sabar in New York.

Finally, I highlighted the need for more research on local conceptions of moving bodies.

Sabar is a tradition, a profession, a hobby, a physical exercise, an outlet for political expression, an environment for community – or even the means to find love, a spouse and a new nationality. Sabar can be a way to make a living or be part of one's project of self-improvement. The more spaces Sabar moves through, the more meanings it acquires in the process. Sabar, however, is more than 'meaning'. As a constellation of pedagogical methods, Sabar structures one's learning and one's access to the world. It reminds us that experience is cultured and of the importance of attending to different ways of learning. We tend to think of pedagogical techniques as access windows to knowledge. As I showed, however, as much as they enable learning, pedagogical techniques also restrict learning. Research remains to be done on local ideas of learning and embodiment, and the different worlds that embodied practices let us access. Exploring what others' techniques can teach us about learning, knowing, the world and ourselves can challenge existing theoretical formulations and offer new insights into the relationship between us, society and culture.

Glossary

baar mbaye: Dance-rhythm of the Sabar repertoire with a slower tempo.

bàkk: Rhythmic phrase used as the basis for improvisation by drummers and dancers.

ballets traditional, folkloric and *semi-folkloric*: Dance companies from Senegal, Guinea and Mali whose repertoire is based on different ethnic traditions of the region. Traditional, folkloric and semi-folkloric denote the orientation of the repertoire and the different degrees of affinity to tradition.

becho: Undergarment. As Sabar involves wide leg movements, the *becho* is worn under a skirt and is revealed when dancing. It is often chosen to contrast in colour with the outer layers of one's clothing so as to attract the audience's attention when dancing.

ceebujen: Translates to rice and fish; popular dish of Senegal and the name of one of the Sabar dance-rhythms with a fast tempo.

créations: From the French *créer* (to create), it is used in reference to the new movements and short 'choreographies' featured and popularized through the videos of the popular music genre *Mbalax*.

Djembé: Name of a drum of the Mandé of West Africa; also used to refer to the West African dances accompanied by the drum.

farwu jar: Dance-rhythm of the Sabar repertoire.

géer: The freeborn, the uncasted.

géwël: The hereditary endogamous group of praise singers, oral historians, musicians and dancers.

griot: Used throughout West Africa and by scholars to denote the 'caste' of praise singers, oral historians, musicians and dancers.

lapa: Used in New York classes to denote a wrap or a sarong worn over one's active gear.

lëmbël: Usually the last dance-rhythm of the Sabar repertoire, characterized by sensual movements.

Mbalax: Popular music genre of Senegal and the name of a drum of the Sabar ensemble. Attributed to musician Youssou NDour, *Mbalax* is characterized by the sounds of synthesizers and electric guitars with the traditional drum ensemble.

pagne: Wrap skirt in Senegal.

Sabar: The name of a Wolof drum, a family of dance-rhythms and the dance-events in which Sabar is performed.

toubaab: Wolof term for those of a Euro-American lifestyle, used initially in reference to the French. It is also used negatively for those Senegalese who are thought to be living by what are perceived to be Western morals and standards of living.

yabba: Dance-rhythm of the Sabar repertoire with a slower tempo.

Bibliography

Abdullah, Z. 2009. 'African "Soul Brothers" in the Hood: Immigration, Islam, and the Black Encounter', *Anthropological Quarterly* 82(1): 37–62.

Angelou, M. 1987. *All God's Children Need Travelling Shoes*. London: Virago.

Appadurai, A. (ed.). 1986. 'Introduction: Commodities and the Politics of Value', in A. Appadurai (ed.), *The Social Life of Things: Commodities in Cultural Perspective*. Cambridge: Cambridge University Press, pp. 3–63.

———. 1990. 'Disjuncture and Difference in the Global Cultural Economy', *Theory, Culture & Society* 7(2): 295–310.

———. 1991. 'Global Ethnoscapes: Notes and Queries for a Transnational Anthropology', in R.G. Fox (ed.), *Recapturing Anthropology: Working in the Present*. Santa Fe: School of American Research Press, pp. 191–210.

Appiah, K.A. 1992. *In My Father's House: Africa in the Philosophy of Culture*. Oxford: Oxford University Press.

———. 1997. 'Europe Upside Down: Fallacies of the New Afrocentrism', in R.R. Grinker and C.B. Steiner (eds), *Perspectives on Africa: A Reader in Culture, History & Representation*. Oxford: Blackwell Publishers, pp. 728–32.

———. 2001. 'African Identities', in G. Castle (ed.), *Postcolonial Discourses: An Anthology*. Massachusetts: Blackwell Publishers, pp. 221–32.

Ardener, E.W. 1975. 'Belief and the Problem of Women', in S. Ardener (ed.), *Perceiving Women*. London: Malaby Press, pp. 1–19.

Ardener, S. 1993. 'Introduction: The Nature of Women in Society', in S. Ardener (ed.), *Defining Females: The Nature of Women in Society*. Oxford: Berg, pp. 1–33.

Askew, K.M. 2002. *Performing the Nation: Swahili Music and Cultural Politics in Tanzania*. Chicago: University of Chicago Press.

Ba, A. 2008. 'Les Femmes Mourides á New York: Une Renégociation de l'Identité Musulmane en Migration', *Le Sénégal des Migrations: Mobilités, Identités et Sociétés*. Paris: Karthala, pp. 389–408.

Babou, C.A. 2002. 'Brotherhood Solidarity, Education and Migration: The Role of the Dahiras among the Murid Muslim Community of New York', *African Affairs* 101: 151–70.

———. 2008. 'Migration, "Caste", Gender, and Social Status among Senegalese Female Hair Braiders in the United States', *Africa Today* 55(2): 3–22.

Barber, K. 1987. 'Popular Arts in Africa', *African Studies Review* 30(3): 1–78.

Berlin, I. 1953. *The Hedgehog and the Fox: An Essay on Tolstoy's View of History*. London: Weidenfeld and Nicolson.

Birdwhistell, R.L. 1970. *Kinesics and Context: Essays on Body Motion Communication.* Philadelphia: University of Pennsylvania Press.

Blacking, J. 1979. 'Introduction', in J. Blacking and J.W. Kealiinohomoku (eds), *The Performing Arts: Music and Dance.* Hague: Mouton Publishers, pp. xiii–xxii.

Bourdieu, P. (1977) 1979. *Outline of a Theory of Practice.* Cambridge: Cambridge University Press.

———. 1990. *In Other Words: Essays Towards a Reflexive Sociology.* Cambridge: Polity.

———. 2004. 'The Peasant and his Body', *Ethnography* 5(4): 579–99.

Bourdieu, P. and J.-C. Passeron. 1977. *Reproduction in Education, Society and Culture.* London: Sage Publications.

Browning, B. 1995. *Samba: Resistance in Motion.* Bloomington: Indiana University Press.

Bruner, E. 1996. 'Tourism in Ghana: The Representation of Slavery and the Return of the Black Diaspora', *American Anthropologist* 98(2): 290–304.

Buckland, T. (ed.). 1999a. *Dance in the Field: Theory, Methods and Issues in Dance Ethnography.* London: St Martin's Press.

———. 1999b. 'All Dances are Ethnic, but Some are More Ethnic than Others: Observations on Dance and Anthropology', *Dance Research* 17(1): 3–21.

Bull, C.J.C. 1997. 'Sense, Meaning, and Perception in Three Dance Cultures', in J.C. Desmond (ed.), *Meaning in Motion: New Cultural Studies of Dance.* Durham, NC: Duke University Press, pp. 269–88.

Carter, D.M. 1997. *States of Grace: Senegalese in Italy and the New European Immigration.* Minneapolis: University of Minnesota Press.

Castaldi, F. 2006. *Choreographies of African Identities: Négritude, Dance and the National Ballet of Senegal.* Urbana: University of Illinois Press.

Chernoff, J.M. 1979. *African Rhythm and African Sensibility: Aesthetics and Social Action in African Musical Idioms.* Chicago: University of Chicago Press.

Classen, C. 1993. *Worlds of Sense: Exploring the Senses in History and across Cultures.* London: Routledge.

Clifford, J. 1992. 'Travelling Cultures', in L. Grossberg, C. Nelson and P. Treichler (eds), *Cultural Studies.* New York: Routledge, pp. 96–116.

———. 1997. *Routes: Travel and Translation in the Late Twentieth Century.* Cambridge: Harvard University Press.

Cohen, A. 1985. *The Symbolic Construction of Community.* Chichester: Ellis Horwood.

Cohen, E. 1988. 'Authenticity and Commoditization in Tourism', *Annals of Tourism Research* 15: 371–86.

———. 1993. 'The Heterogenization of Tourist Art', *Annals of Tourism Research* 20: 138–63.

Conrad, D.C. and B.E. Frank. 1995. 'Introduction Nyamakalaya: Contradiction and Ambiguity in Mande Society', in C.D. Conrad and B.E. Frank (eds), *Status and Identity in West Africa: Nyamakalaw of Mande.* Bloomington: Indiana University Press, pp. 1–23.

Conrad, J. (1899) 1994. *Heart of Darkness.* Harmondsworth: Penguin.

Coombe, R.J. and P. Stoller. 1994. 'X Marks the Spot: The Ambiguities of African Trading in the Commerce of the Black Public Sphere', *Public Culture* 7(1): 249–74.

Coombes, A.E. 1994. *Reinventing Africa: Museums, Material Culture and Popular Imagination in Late Victorian and Edwardian England.* London: Yale University Press.

Coulon, C. and D. Cruise O'Brien. 1989. 'Senegal', in *Contemporary West African States*, D. Cruise O'Brien, J. Dunn and R. Rathbone (eds). Cambridge: Cambridge University Press, pp. 145–64.

Cowan, J.K. 1990. *Dance and the Body Politic in Northern Greece*. Princeton: Princeton University Press.

Coy, M.W. (ed.). 1989. *Apprenticeship: From Theory to Method and Back Again*. Albany: State University of New York Press.

Crick, M. 1989. 'Representations of International Tourism in the Social Sciences: Sun, Sex, Sights, Savings, and Servility', *Annual Review of Anthropology* 18: 307–44.

Crossley, N. 2004. 'The Circuit Trainer's Habitus: Reflexive Body Techniques and the Sociality of the Workout', *Body & Society* 10(1): 37–69.

Crowder, M. 1968. *West Africa under Colonial Rule*. Evanston, IL: Northwestern University Press.

Csordas, T.J. 1990. 'Embodiment as a Paradigm for Anthropology', *Ethos* 18: 5–47.

———. 1993. 'Somatic Modes of Attention', *Cultural Anthropology* 8(2): 135–36.

———. 1994. 'Introduction: The Body as Representation and Being-in-the-World', in T.J. Csordas (ed.), *Embodiment and Experience: The Existential Ground of Culture and Self.* Cambridge: Cambridge University Press, pp. 1–26.

———. 1999. 'The Body's Career in Anthropology', in H.L. Moore (ed.), *Anthropological Theory Today*. Cambridge: Polity Press, pp. 172–205.

Daniel, Y. 1995. *Rumba: Dance and Social Change in Contemporary Cuba*. Bloomington: Indiana University Press.

Davidson, B. (with F.K. Buah and the advice of J.F. Ade Ajayi). 1966. *A History of West Africa: To the Nineteenth Century*. New York: Anchor Books.

DeFrantz, F.T. 2002. 'African American Dance: A Complex History', in F.T. DeFrantz (ed.), *Dancing Many Drums: Excavations in African American Dance*. Madison: University of Wisconsin Press, pp. 3–38.

Desforges, L. 2000. 'Travelling the World: Identity and Travel Biography', *Annals of Tourism Research* 27(4): 926–45.

Diallo, P.I. 2009. *Les Guinéens de Dakar: Migration et Intégration en Afrique de l'Ouest*. Paris: L'Harmattan.

Dilley, R.M. 1989. 'Secrets and Skills: Apprenticeship amongst Tukolor Weavers', in M.W. Coy (ed.), *Apprenticeship: From Theory to Method and Back Again*. Albany: State University of New York Press, pp. 181–98.

——— (ed.). 1999a. 'Introduction: The Problem of Context', in *The Problem of Context*. Oxford: Berghahn Books, pp. 1–46.

———. 1999b. 'Ways of Knowing, Forms of Power', *Cultural Dynamics* 11(1): 33–55.

———. 2000. 'The Question of "Caste" in West Africa with Special Reference to Tukulor Craftsmen', *Anthropos* 95(1): 149–65.

Diop, A.-B. 1981. *La Société Wolof. Tradition and Changement: Les Systèmes d'Inégalité et de Domination*. Paris: Karthala.

Diop, C.A. 1997. 'The Meaning of Our Work', in R.R. Grinker and C.B. Steiner (eds), *Perspectives on Africa: A Reader in Culture, History & Representation*. Oxford: Blackwell Publishers, pp. 724–28.

Dixon-Gottschild, B. 1996. *Digging the Africanist Present in American Performance*. Westport: Greenwood.

———. 2003. *The Black Dancing Body: A Geography from Coon to Cool*. New York: Palgrave Macmillan.

Djembefola. 1991. Documentary, directed by Laurent Chevallier [DVD]. USA: Interama Video.

Dobbin, J.D. 1986. *The Jombee Dance of Montserrat: A Study of Trance Ritual in the West Indies*. Columbus: Ohio State University Press.

Douglas, M. 1973. *Natural Symbols: Explorations in Cosmology*. London: Barrie and Jenkins.

Downey, G. 2005. *Learning Capoeira: Lessons in Cunning from an Afro-Brazilian Art*. Oxford: Oxford University Press.

Drewal, M.T. 1989. 'Dancing for Ogun in Yorubaland and in Brazil', in S.T. Barnes (ed.), *Africa's Ogun: Old World and New*. Bloomington: Indiana University Press, pp. 199–234.

Dunham, K. 1969. *Island Possessed*. Chicago: University of Chicago Press.

Duran, L. 1989. 'Key to N'Dour: Roots of the Senegalese Star', *Popular Music* 8(3): 275–84.

Dyck, N. and E.P. Archetti (eds). 2003. *Sport, Dance and Embodied Identities*. Oxford: Berg.

Ebron, P.A. 2002. *Performing Africa*. Princeton: Princeton University Press.

Economist. 1994. 'Only in Afro-America', *Economist* 333(7894): A32.

Emery, L.F. (1972) 1988. *Black Dance: From 1619 to Today*. Pennington: Princeton Book Company.

Essien, K. 2008. 'African Americans in Ghana and their Contributions to "Nation Building" since 1985', in A. Jalloh and T. Falola (eds), *The United States and West Africa: Interactions and Relations*. Rochester: University of Rochester Press, pp. 147–73.

Evans-Pritchard, E.E. 1928. 'The Dance', *Africa* 1: 446–62.

Fabre, G. and R. O'Meally (eds). 1994. 'Introduction', in *History and Memory in African-American Culture*. New York: Oxford University Press, pp. 3–17.

Fanon, F. 1963. *The Wretched of the Earth*. London: Penguin Books.

———. (1952) 1986. *Black Skin White Masks*. London: Pluto Press.

Farnell, B. 1996 'Metaphors We Move By', *Visual Anthropology* 8(2–4): 331–35.

———. 1999. 'Moving Bodies, Acting Selves', *Annual Review of Anthropology* 28: 341–73.

———. 2000. 'Getting Out of the Habitus: An Anthropological Model of Dynamically Embodied Social Action', *Journal of the Royal Anthropological Institute* 6(3): 397–418.

Farnell, B. and C.R. Varela. 2008. 'The Second Somatic Revolution', *Journal for the Theory of Social Behaviour* 38(3): 215–40.

Feld, S. and K.H. Basso (eds). 1996. 'Introduction', in *Senses of Place*. Santa Fe: School of American Research Press, pp. 3–12.

Ferguson, J. 1988. 'Review: Cultural Exchange: New Developments in the Anthropology of Commodities' [Reviewed work(s): 'The Social Life of Things: Commodities in Cultural Perspective' by Arjun Appadurai] *Cultural Anthropology* 3(4): 488–513.

Foner, N. (ed.). 2001. 'Introduction: West Indian Migration to New York: An Overview', in *Islands in the City: West Indian Migration to New York*. Berkeley: University of California Press, pp. 1–21.

Foster, S.L. 2011. *Choreographing Empathy: Kinaesthesia in Performance*. New York: Routledge.

Foucault, M. 1980. C. (ed., trans.) *Power-Knowledge: Selected Interviews and Other Writings, 1972–1977*. Brighton: Harvester Press.

Frankland, S. 2001. 'Pygmic Tours', *African Study Monographs* 26(1): 237–56.

Gell, A. 1998. *Art and Agency: An Anthropological Theory*. New York: Oxford University Press.

Geurts, K.L. 2002. *Culture and the Senses: Bodily Ways of Knowing in an African Community*. Berkeley: University of California Press.

Ghosh, A. 1994. 'The Imam and the Indian', in A. Bammer (ed.), *Displacements: Cultural Identities in Question*. Bloomington: Indiana University Press, pp. 47–56.

———. 1998. *In an Antique Land*. London: Granta.

Gibson, J.J. 1979. *The Ecological Approach to Visual Perception*. Boston: Houghton Mifflin.

Gilman, L. 2009. *The Dance of Politics: Gender, Performance, and Democratization in Malawi*. Philadelphia: Temple University Press.

Gilroy, P. 1986. *'There Ain't no Black in the Union Jack': The Cultural Politics of Race and Nation*. London: Hutchinson.

———. 1993. *The Black Atlantic: Modernity and Double Consciousness*. London: Verso.

Grau, A. 1993. 'John Blacking and the Development of Dance Anthropology in the UK', *Dance Research Journal* 25(2): 21–31.

———. 2003. 'Tiwi Dance Aesthetics', *Yearbook for Traditional Music* 35: 173–78.

Gupta, A. and J. Ferguson. 1992. 'Beyond "Culture": Space, Identity, and the Politics of Difference', *Cultural Anthropology* 7(1): 6–23.

Haley, A. 1966. *The Autobiography of Malcolm X: As Told to Alex Haley*. New York: Grove.

Hall, E.T. 1969. *The Hidden Dimension*. New York: Doubleday.

Hall, M.C. and C. Ryan. 2001. *Sex Tourism: Marginal People and Liminalities*. New York: Routledge.

Handler, R. 1988. *Nationalism and the Politics of Culture in Quebec*. Madison: University of Wisconsin Press.

Hanks, W.F. 1991. 'Foreword', in L. Jean and E. Wenger (eds), *Situated Learning: Legitimate Peripheral Participation*. Cambridge: Cambridge University Press, pp. 13–24.

Hannerz, U. 1989. 'Notes on the Global Ecumene', *Public Culture* 1(2): 66–75.

———. 1997. 'Flows, Boundaries and Hybrids: Keywords in Transnational Anthropology', *Mana* 3(1): 7–39.

———. 2003. 'Several Sites in One', in T.H. Eriksen (ed.), *Globalisation: Studies in Anthropology*. London: Pluto Press, pp. 18–38.

———. 2004. *Foreign News: Exploring the World of Foreign Correspondents*. Chicago: University of Chicago Press.

Hargreaves, J.D. 1963. *Prelude to the Partition of West Africa*. London: Macmillan.

Harkin, M. 1995. 'Modernist Anthropology and Tourism of the Authentic', *Annals of Tourism Research* 22(3): 650–70.

Harris, M. 2005. 'Riding a Wave: Embodied Skills and Colonial History on the Amazon Floodplain', *Ethnos* 70(2): 197–219.

Harshe, R. 1984. 'Guinea under Sékou Touré', *Economic and Political Weekly* 19(15): 624–26

Hart, K. 1982. 'On Commoditization', in E. Goody (ed.), *From Craft to Industry: The Ethnography of Proto-Industrial Cloth Production*. Cambridge: Cambridge University Press, pp. 38–49.

Hazzard-Gordon, K. 1985. 'African-American Vernacular Dance: Core-Culture and Meaning Operatives', *Journal of Black Studies* 15(4): 427–45.

———. 1990. *The Rise of Social Dance Formations in African-American Culture*. Philadelphia: Temple University Press.

Heard, M.E. and M.K. Mussa. 2002. 'African Dance in New York City', in T.F. DeFrantz (ed.), *Dancing Many Drums: Excavations in African American Dance*. Madison: University of Wisconsin Press, pp. 143–68.

Heath, D. 1994. 'The Politics of Appropriateness and Appropriation: Recontextualizing Women's Dance in Urban Senegal', *American Ethnologist* 21(1): 88–103.

Herold, E., R. Garcia and T. DeMoya. 2001. 'Female Tourists and Beach Boys: Romance or Sex Tourism?', *Annals of Tourism Research* 28(4): 978–97.

Herzfeld, M. 1991. 'Silence, Submission and Subversion: Towards a Poetics of Womanhood', in P. Loizos and E. Papataxiarxhis (eds), *Contested Identities: Gender and Kinship in Modern Greece*. Princeton: Princeton University Press, pp. 79–97.

Hobart, M. 1986. 'Introduction: Context, Meaning, and Power', in M. Hobart and R.H. Taylor (eds), *Context, Meaning, and Power in Southeast Asia*. Ithaca, NY: Cornell University, pp. 7–10.

Howes, D. (ed.). 1991. *The Varieties of Sensory Experience: A Sourcebook in the Anthropology of the Senses*. Toronto: University of Toronto Press.

Hymans, J.L. 1971. *Léopold Sédar Senghor: An Intellectual Biography*. Edinburgh: Edinburgh University Press.

Ingold, T. 2000. *The Perception of the Environment: Essays on Livelihood, Dwelling and Skill*. London: Routledge.

———. 2008. 'Anthropology is *Not* Ethnography', *Proceedings of the British Academy* 154: 69–92.

International Organization for Migration (IOM). 2009. Migration au Sénégal: Profil National 2009. www.iom.int

Irvine, J.T. 1974. '"Caste" and Communication in a Wolof Village'. Ph.D. dissertation. Philadelphia: University of Pennsylvania.

Jackson, M. 1983. 'Knowledge of the Body', *Man* 18(2): 327–45.

Jenkins, T.J. 1995. 'Misguided "Authenticity"', *American Visions* 10(2): 4.

Johnson, R.W. 1978. 'Guinea', in John Dunn (ed.), *West African States: Failure and Promise*, Cambridge: Cambridge University Press, pp. 66–116.

Johnson, R., Jr. 1999. *Why Blacks Left America for Africa: Interviews with Black Repatriates, 1971–1999*. Westport, CT: Praeger.

Kaeppler, A.L. 1971. 'Aesthetics of Tongan Dance', *Ethnomusicology* 15(2): 175–85.

———. 1972. 'Method and Theory in Analyzing Dance Structure with an Analysis of Tongan Dance', *Ethnomusicology* 16(2): 173–217.

———. 2000. 'Dance Ethnology and the Anthropology of Dance', *Dance Research Journal* 32(1): 116–25.

———. 2003. 'An Introduction to Dance Aesthetics', *Yearbook for Traditional Music* 35: 153–62.

Kealiinohomoku, J.W. 1973. *Cultural Change: Functional and Dysfunctional Expressions of Dance, a Form of Affective Culture*. IX International Conference of Anthropological and Ethnological Sciences, Chicago.

————. 1976. 'A Comparative Study of Dance as a Constellation of Motor Behaviours among African and United States Negroes', in A.L. Kaeppler (ed.) *Reflection and Perspectives on Two Anthropological Studies of Dance*. New York: CORD Dance Research Annual 7: 1–179.

Krauss, C. 1994. 'Offering Shelter from the Storm of the Streets', *The New York Times*, 20 August.

Kubik, G. 1979. 'Pattern Perception and Recognition in African Music', in J. Blacking and J. Kealiinohomoku (eds), *The Performing Arts: Music and Dance*. The Hague: Mouton Publishers, pp. 221–50.

Kurath, G.P. 1957. 'Dance–Music Interdependence', *Ethnomusicology* 1(10): 8–11.

————. 1960. 'Panorama of Dance Ethnology', *Current Anthropology* 1(3): 233–54.

Kuyk, B.M. 2003. *African Voices in the African American Heritage*. Bloomington: Indiana University Press.

Lave, J. 1990. 'The Culture of Acquisition and the Practice of Understanding', in J.W. Stigler, R.A. Scweder and G. Herdt (eds), *Cultural Psychology: Essays on Comparative Human Development*. Cambridge: Cambridge University Press, pp. 309–27.

Lave, J. and E. Wenger 1991. *Situated Learning: Legitimate Peripheral Participation*. Cambridge: Cambridge University Press.

Leder, D. 1990. *The Absent Body*. Chicago: University of Chicago Press.

Lock, M. 1993. 'Cultivating the Body: Anthropology and Epistemologies of Bodily Practice and Knowledge', *Annual Review of Anthropology* 22: 133–55.

Locke, D. 1982. 'Principles of Offbeat Timing and Cross-Rhythm in Southern Eve Dance Drumming', *Ethnomusicology* 26(2): 217–46.

Lopez, R. and I. Hathie. 1998. 'Structural Adjustment Programs and Peanut Market Performance in Senegal'. American Agricultural Economics Association Annual Meeting, 2–5 August, Salt Lake City, UT.

Mabogunje, A.L. 1971. 'The Land and Peoples of West Africa', in J.F. Ade Ajayi and Michael Crowder (eds), *History of West Africa, Vol. 1*. New York: Columbia University Press, pp. 1–32.

MacCannell, D. 1976. *The Tourist: A New Theory of the Leisure Class*. London: Macmillian.

Malcomson, S.L. 1996. 'West of Eden', *Transitions* 71: 24–43.

Malone, J. 1996. *The Visible Rhythms of African American Dance: Steppin' on the Blues*. Urbana: University of Illinois Press.

Marcus, G.E. 1995. 'Ethnography in/of the World System: The Emergence of Multi-Sited Ethnography', *Annual Review of Anthropology* 24: 95–117.

Mark, P. 1994. 'Art, Ritual and Folklore: Dance and Cultural Identity among the Peoples of the Casamance', *Cahiers d'Etudes Africaines* 136: 563–84.

Markovitz, I.L. 1969. *Léopold Sédar Senghor and the Politics of Négritude*. New York: Atheneum.

Marx, K. (1887) 1971. *Capital: Vol. I. A Critical Analysis of Capitalist Production*. Moscow: Progress Publishers.

Mauss, M. (1922) 1976. *The Gift*. New York: Norton.

————. (1935) 1979. 'Body Techniques', *Sociology and Psychology: Essays*. London: Routledge & Kegan Paul, pp. 97–123.

Mayer, R. 2002. *Artificial Africas: Colonial Images in the Times of Globalization*. Hanover, NH: University Press of New England.

Meillasoux, C. 1991. *The Anthropology of Slavery: The Womb of Iron and Gold*. Chicago: The University of Chicago Press.

Mekuria, W. 2006. 'Modern-day Griots: Imagining Africa, Choreographing Experience, in a West African Performance in New York', Ph.D. dissertation. New York: City University of New York.

Miller, D. 1995. 'Consumption and Commodities', *Annual Review of Anthropology* 24: 141–61.

Mintz, S.W. 1998. 'The Localization of Anthropological Practice: From Area Studies to Transnationalism', *Critique of Anthropology* 18(2): 117–33.

Mudimbe, V.Y. 1988. *The Invention of Africa: Gnosis, Philosophy and the Order of Knowledge*. Bloomington: Indiana University Press.

Munt, I. 1994. 'Eco-tourism or Ego-tourism?', *Race Class* 36: 49–60.

Ndiaye, A.I. 2008. 'Dakar et ses Etrangers: La Construction Politique et Sociale de la Cohabitation Communautaire', in M.-C. Diop (ed.), *Le Sénégal des Migrations: Mobilités, Identités et Sociétés*. Paris: Karthala, pp. 409–32.

Ness, S.A. 1992. *Body, Movement, and Culture: Kinaesthetic and Visual Symbolism in a Philippine Community*. Philadelphia: University of Pennsylvania Press.

Neveu Kringelbach, H. 2005. 'Encircling the Dance: Social Mobility through the Transformation of Performance in Urban Senegal', Ph.D. dissertation. Oxford: University of Oxford.

Newbury, C.W. and A.S. Kanya-Forstner. 1969. 'French Policy and the Origins of the Scramble for West Africa', *Journal of African History* 10(2): 253–76.

Nicholls, R. 1996. 'African Dance: Transition and Continuity', in K. Welsh-Asante (ed.), *African Dance: An Artistic, Historical, and Philosophical Inquiry*. Trenton, NJ: African World Press, pp. 41–62.

Novack, C. 1990. *Sharing the Dance: Contact Improvisation and American Culture*. Madison: The University of Wisconsin Press.

Oppermann, M. 1999. 'Sex Tourism', *Annals of Tourism Research* 26(2): 251–66.

Orbe, M.P. 1995. 'African American Communication Research: Toward a Deeper Understanding of Interethnic Communication', *Western Journal of Communication* 59: 61–78.

Orbe, M.P. and T.M. Harris. 2008. *Interracial Communication: Theory into Practice*. Thousand Oaks, CA: Sage Publications.

Ortner, S. 1984. 'Theory in Anthropology since the Sixties', *Comparative Studies in Society and History* 26(1): 126–66.

Pálsson, G. 1994. 'Enskilment at Sea', *Man* 29(4): 901–27.

Panzacchi, C. 1994. 'The Livelihoods of Traditional Griots in Modern Senegal', *Africa* 64(2): 190–210.

Perry, D.L. 1997. 'Rural Ideologies and Urban Imaginings: Wolof Immigrants in New York City', *Africa Today* 44(2): 229–60.

Polanyi, M. (1958) 1973. *Personal Knowledge: Towards a Post-critical Philosophy*. London: Routledge & Kegan Paul.

Polgreen, L. 2007. 'Discontent in Guinea Nears Boiling Point', *New York Times*, 20 February.

Potter, C. 2008. 'Sense of Motion, Senses of Self: Becoming a Dancer', *Ethnos* 73(4): 444–65.

Pruitt, D. and S. LaFont. 2001. 'For Love and Money: Romance Tourism in Jamaica', *Annals of Tourism Research* 22(2): 422–40.

Rada, A.D. de and F. Cruces. 1994. 'The Mysteries of Incarnation: Some Problems to Do with the Analytic Language of Practice', in K. Hastrup and P. Hervik (eds), *Social Experience and Anthropological Knowledge*. London: Routledge, pp. 101–20.

Ramsey, K. 1997. 'Vodou, Nationalism, and Performance: The Staging of Folklore in Mid-Twentieth-Century Haiti', in J.C. Desmond (ed.), *Meaning in Motion: New Cultural Studies of Dance*. Durham, NC: Duke University Press, pp. 345–78.

———. 2000. 'Melville Herskovits, Katherine Dunham, and the Politics of African Diasporic Dance Anthropology', in L. Doolittle and A. Flynn (eds), *Dancing Bodies, Living Histories: New Writings about Dance and Culture*. Banff: Banff Centre Press, pp. 197–216.

Reed, D.B. 2003. *Dan Ge Performance: Masks and Music in Contemporary Côte d'Ivoire*. Bloomington: Indiana University Press.

Reed, S.A. 1998. 'The Politics and Poetics of Dance', *Annual Review of Anthropology* 27: 503–32.

Reisinger, Y. and C.J. Steiner. 2006a. 'Reconceptualizing Object Authenticity', *Annals of Tourism Research* 53(1): 65–86.

———. 2006b. 'Understanding Existential Authenticity', *Annals of Tourism Research* 33(2): 299–318.

Rogoff, B. 1990. *Apprenticeship in Thinking: Cognitive Development in Social Context*. Oxford: Oxford University Press.

Rouch, J. 1956. 'Migrations au Ghana (Gold Coast: enquête 1953–1955)', *Journal de la Société des Africanistes* 26(1–2): 33–196.

———. 1972. *Horendi*. Film Documentary.

Rouget, G. (1980) 1985. *Music and Trance: A Theory of the Relations between Music and Possession*. Chicago: The University of Chicago Press.

Royce, A.P. 1977. *The Anthropology of Dance*. Bloomington: Indiana University Press.

———. 1997. 'Extract #1, Extract #2', in D. Williams (ed.), *Anthropology and Human Movement: The Study of Dances*. New York: The Scarecrow Press, pp. 38–51.

Schieffelin, E.L. 1976. *The Sorrow of the Lonely and the Burning of the Dancers*. New York: St Martin's Press.

Schmidt, E. 2005. 'Top Down or Bottom Up? Nationalist Mobilization Reconsidered, with Special Reference to Guinea (French West Africa)', *The American Historical Review* 110(4): 975–1014.

Schulz, D.A. 2001. 'Music Videos and the Effeminate Vices of Urban Culture in Mali', *Africa* 71(3): 345–72.

Seabrook, J. 1996. *Travels in the Skin Trade*. London: Pluto Press.

Searing, F.J. 1988. 'Aristocrats, Slaves, and Peasants: Power and Dependency in the Wolof States, 1700–1850', *The International Journal of African Historical Studies* 21(3): 475–503.

Senghor, L.S. 1970. 'Négritude: A Humanism of the Twentieth Century', in W. Cartey and M. Kilson (eds), *The Africa Reader: Independent Africa*. Vintage Books: New York, pp. 179–92.

Sigaut, F. 1993. 'Learning, Teaching, and Apprenticeship', *New Literary History* 24(1): 105–14.

Sklar, D. 2000. 'Reprise: On Dance Ethnography', *Dance Research Journal* 32(1): 70–77.

———. 2008. 'Remembering Kinaesthesia: An Inquiry into Embodied Cultural Knowledge', in C. Noland and S.A. Ness (eds), *Migrations of Gesture*. Minneapolis: University of Minesota Press, pp. 85–112.

Stearns, J. 1994. *Jazz Dance: The Story of American Vernacular Dance*. New York: Da Capo Press.

Stilitoe, P. 2003. *Managing Animals in New Guinea: Preying the Game in the Highlands*. New York: Routledge.

Stoller, P. 1989. *The Taste of Ethnographic Things: The Senses in Anthropology*. Philadelphia: University of Pennsylvania Press.

———. 1992. *The Cinematic Griot: The Ethnography of Jean Rouch*. Chicago: University of Chicago Press.

———. 1997. 'Globalising Method: The Problem of Doing Ethnography in Transnational Spaces', *Anthropology and Humanism* 22(1): 81–94.

———. 2002. *Money Has No Smell: The Africanization of New York City*. Chicago: University of Chicago Press.

———. 2004. *Stranger in the Village of the Sick: A Memoir of Cancer, Sorcery and Healing*. Boston: Beacon Press.

Stoller, P. and C. Olkes. 1987. *In Sorcery's Shadow: A Memoir of Apprenticeship among the Songhay of Niger*. Chicago: University of Chicago Press.

Straker, J. 2007. 'Stories of "Militant Theatre" in the Guinean Forest: "Demystifying" the Motives and Moralities of a Revolutionary Nation-State', *Journal of African Cultural Studies* 19(2): 207–33.

Sunkett, M. 1995. *Mandiani Drum and Dance: Djimbe Performance and Black Aesthetics from Africa to the New World*. Arizona: White Cliffs Media.

Tamari, T. 1991. 'The Development of "Caste" Systems in West Africa', *The Journal of African History* 32(2): 221–50.

Tang, P. 2007. *Masters of the Sabar: Wolof Griot Percussionists of Senegal*. Philadelphia, PA: Temple University Press.

The World Factbook 2009. Washington, DC: Central Intelligence Agency. https://www.cia.gov/library/publications/the-world-factbook/index.html [retrieved 19 March 2011].

Thompson, R.F. 1966. 'An Aesthetic of the Cool: West African Dance', *African Forum* 2(2): 85–102.

Truong, T.-D. 1990. *Sex, Money and Morality: Prostitution and Tourism in South East Asia*. London: Zed.

Tsing, A. 2000. 'The Global Situation', *Cultural Anthropology* 15(3): 327–60.

Turnbull, C.M. 1983. *The Mbuti Pygmies: Change and Adaptation*. London: Holt, Rinehart and Winston.

Urry, J. 1990. *The Tourist Gaze: Leisure and Travel in Contemporary Societies*. London: Sage.

———. 1995. *Consuming Places*. London: Routledge.

U.S. Citizenship and Immigration Services. www.uscis.gov. Retrieved 31 January 2011.

Vygotsky, L.S. 1978. *Mind in Society: The Development of Higher Psychological Processes*. Cambridge, MA: Harvard University Press.

Wacquant, L.J.D. 1995. 'The Pugilistic Point of View: How Boxers Think and Feel about their Trade', *Theory and Society* 24(4): 489–535.

———. 2004. *Body and Soul: Ethnographic Notebooks of an Apprentice Boxer*. New York: Oxford University Press.

Walker, S.S. 2001. *African Roots/American Cultures: Africa in the Creation of the Americas*. Maryland: Rowman and Littlefield Publishers Inc.

Waters, M.C. 1999. *Black Identities: West Indian Immigrant Dreams and American Realities*. New York: Russell Sage Foundation.

White, B.W. 2008. *Rumba Rules: The Politics of Dance Music in Mobutu's Zaire*. Durham, NC: Duke University Press.

Wilkinson, A.D. 1996. 'Afrocentric Marketing is Not Just a Niche', *Black Enterprise* 26(12): 72–77.

Williams, D. 1997. *Anthropology and the Human Movement: The Study of Dances*. New York: The Scarecrow Press.

———. (1991) 2004. *Anthropology and the Dance: Ten Lectures*. Urbana: University of Illinois Press.

Wober, M. 1991. 'The Sensotype Hypothesis', in D. Howes (ed.) *The Varieties of Sensory Experience: A Sourcebook in the Anthropology of the Senses*. Toronto: University of Toronto Press, pp. 31–42.

World Bank Migration and Remittance Factbook 2011. Retrieved on 13 September 2012. http://siteresources.worldbank.org/INTPROSPECTS/Resources/334934-1199 807908806/Guinea.pdf

Wright, B.L. 1989. 'The Power of Articulation', in W. Arens and I. Karp (eds), *Creativity of Power: Cosmology and Action in African Societies*. London: Smithsonian Institution Press, pp. 39–58.

Wulff, H. 1998. *Ballet across Boarders: Career and Culture in the World of Dancers*. Oxford: Berg.

———. 2000. 'Access to a Closed World: Methods for a Multilocale Study on Ballet as a Career', in V. Amit (ed.), *Constructing the Field: Ethnographic Fieldwork in the Contemporary World*. London: Routledge, pp. 147–61.

———. 2002. 'Aesthetics at the Ballet: Looking at "National" Style, Body and Clothing in the London Dance World', in N. Rapport (ed.), *British Subjects: An Anthropology of Britain*. Oxford: Berg, pp. 67–86.

———. 2003. 'The Irish Body in Motion: Moral Politics, National Identity and Dance', in N. Dyck and E.P. Archetti (eds), *Sport, Dance and Embodied Identities*. Oxford: Berg, pp. 179–96.

———. 2007. *Dancing at the Crossroads: Memory and Mobility in Ireland*. Oxford: Berghahn Books.

Index